Tactical Attitude

By

Phil L. Duran and Dennis Nasci

LOOSELEAF LAW
PUBLICATIONS, INC.
43-08 162nd Street
Flushing, New York 11358

Library of Congress Cataloging-in-Publication Data

Duran, Phil L.
    Tactical attitude / by Phil L. Duran and Dennis Nasci.
       p. cm.
    Includes bibliographical references and index.
    ISBN 1-889031-40-2 (paperback)
    1. Police patrol. 2. Police–Violence against–Prevention. 3. Police murders–Prevention. 4. Self-preservation. 5. Self-defense. 6. Self-protective behavior. I. Nasci, Dennis, 1957- II. Title.

HV8080.P2 D87 2000
363.2'3'028--dc21

                            00-063480

Acknowledgments

The authors would like to thank all the law enforcement officers who so willingly shared their experiences. This book would not have been possible without their openness and candor.

The **Officer Survival Creed** is dedicated to Phil Duran and Dennis Nasci and the work they do in striving to keep law enforcement officers safe.

Peter M. Lopez, Veteran Officer
Los Angeles Police Department

Our thanks to Bruce Ford for his inspiring cover design. In so doing, he has incorporated a tribute to officers that have fallen.

About the Authors

Phil Duran has been a law enforcement officer since 1988. He is the author of *Developing the Survival Attitude, A Guide for the New Officer*. He has been published in Law and Order Magazine on the subject of Officer Survival. He is certified by the state of New Mexico as an Officer Survival instructor. He has received training in Officer Survival from the Federal Bureau of Investigation, the New Mexico Law Enforcement Academy, and the Bernalillo County Sheriff's Department. He holds an instructor certificate in Officer Survival from the Metropolitan Police Institute in Miami, Florida. He has instructed Officer Survival and other law enforcement subjects for the Bernalillo County Sheriff's Department Regional Law Enforcement Academy, the Bernalillo County Sheriff's Department Reserve Academy, Bureau of Indian Affairs and the New Mexico Mounted Patrol. Phil Duran is also certified by the state of New Mexico as an instructor in general police subjects, bombs and explosives, and booby trap devices. His experience includes patrol, child abuse and sex crime investigations, fugitive investigations, court services, recruiting, and academy assignments. He knows first hand what it means to be involved in a critical incident, and what it takes to survive, including the importance of the proper attitude and how it relates to survival.

Dennis Nasci has been a law enforcement officer since 1981. He is certified by the State of New Mexico as an instructor in Officer Survival, accident investigation, background investigation, firearms, SWAT, and general police subjects. He has instructed Officer Survival and other police subjects at the Bernalillo County Sheriff's Department Regional Law Enforcement Academy since 1983, as well as at the New Mexico Law Enforcement Academy. Dennis Nasci is a graduate of the 190th session of the F.B.I. National Academy, and a graduate of the D.E.A.'s Drug Unit Commanders Academy. He has commanded a number of units, which include Narcotics, Homicide, Child Abuse, Sex Crimes, White Collar Crimes, and Federal Task Forces. He has also served as an Assistant Division Commander (Criminal Investigations Division), and Field Services Division Watch Commander. He has served as a Criminalistics Supervisor,

Patrol Supervisor, Traffic Accident Investigation Unit Supervisor, and a Hiring, Recruiting, and Training supervisor. He has SWAT Team experience as an Element Leader and an Assistant Commander. Additional experience includes Patrol, Court Services, Range Master and Range Officer Assignments. Dennis Nasci has completed numerous advanced training courses conducted by IPTM, Northwestern University, IACP, California POST, the US Department of Justice, the US Department of Energy, the New Mexico Law Enforcement Academy, and the Bernalillo County Sheriff's Department, among others. In his many years of law enforcement experience he has personally been involved in numerous high stress, high risk situations in both uniform and non-uniform assignments. Dennis Nasci believes that the proper survival attitude, a constant review of officer survival skills, an open mind to new teachings, and the practicing of all skills (old and new) are responsible for the outcome of all of his known and unknown risk encounters.

Table of Contents

Introduction

As you know, after a certain amount of time in the law enforcement profession, it can be very easy to become complacent where survival is concerned. Although law enforcement officers know that police work is dangerous, this still occurs. Of course, not all officers become complacent in their use of tactics. Some continually work to maintain and/or improve their survival skills. But even the most survival minded officers know that after months or years in law enforcement, complacency can be difficult to fight.

What is it that makes us complacent? It might be a result of the false sense of security that develops when officers respond to call after call without ever becoming involved in a life or death encounter. Perhaps in some cases it's a result of officers refusing to believe they could be seriously injured or killed in the line of duty. Many people, including some officers, just don't want to think about death, and to study or practice survival skills is to admit vulnerability. Regardless of what causes it, complacency is something all law enforcement officers must battle on a daily basis. By writing this book it is our hope to give the seasoned officer a renewed commitment to tactical thinking and survival.

An experience of one of the authors, Phil Duran, illustrates the need for officers to be aware of the dangers of complacency. It also reminds us that tactical thinking can go a long way toward helping you to survive when a situation goes bad.

My partner and I were assigned to pick up a subject on an emergency mental health commitment order. The lieutenant who gave us the assignment didn't give us very much information. All we knew was that the subject was supposed to be very unstable and he had been carrying a gun with him everywhere he went. When the paperwork was ready, we went downtown to pick it up. When we got there, the lieutenant was leaving with the father of the subject that we were supposed to pick up. The sergeant was there too, and he said that the lieutenant and the father were going to go in first, and we were supposed to follow a couple of minutes later. The idea was that because the lieutenant was in plain clothes, he and the subject's father might be able to keep the subject calm and convince him to go with us peacefully. The subject's father said that if the subject saw uniformed deputies walk in, he might start shooting. I didn't like the plan. The idea of the lieutenant going in by himself was not safe. Nor did I like the idea of taking a civilian into a potentially violent situation, regardless of his relationship to the subject. But because everyone was on the way out of the building when we got there, I didn't get a chance to say anything before we left the station. As it turned out, it didn't matter because my partner and I arrived a couple of minutes after the lieutenant anyway.

When we got to the subject's residence, the sergeant was waiting outside. He told us that the lieutenant and the subject's father had been inside for about two minutes, so we went into the house. The lieutenant and the father were standing in the living room with the subject sitting on the floor in front of them. They were telling him about the order and trying to convince him to go with us. He just kept telling them to leave. The subject was sitting behind a barricade that he had made out of bricks. At the time I didn't even realize that it was a barricade. I just thought it was part of the house. I wasn't really looking at it. I was looking around the room, trying to locate the gun. The only thing that concerned me about the wall was the fact that the subject was almost completely hidden behind it. I couldn't see his hands, a critical factor where officer survival is concerned. But the lieutenant was in a position to see the subject's hands and he didn't seem to be concerned about his safety at all. He was standing very casually while talking to the subject, so I figured the gun must be hidden somewhere. Based on the minimal information we had received, I figured the gun had to be close by the subject, but I thought there was no way it could be in plain view, or else the lieutenant would not have been standing there so casually. I wanted to get into a position to be able to see the subject's hands but there was nowhere to go. The room was small and with the barricade that the subject had built, the only way to get into a position to see his hands would have been to go around the lieutenant

iv

and the subject's father, and approach from the other side. There just wasn't room to do it without drawing the subject's attention away from the conversation and possibly agitating the subject further. Not wanting to escalate the situation, I decided my best bet would be to stay where I was and be a cover officer. I didn't draw my weapon because I assumed that if the subject's weapon was visible, the lieutenant would not be standing right in front of the subject with his weapon holstered.

The lieutenant and the father were still talking to the subject and he was still telling us to leave. I remember him saying, "I'm prepared to shoot to defend myself." At this point my partner stepped forward to say something and the subject yelled, "No!" and I saw the lieutenant go for his gun. As I was drawing my weapon, I heard two shots. They didn't sound very loud at all. They were just muffled pops. As I was bringing my weapon up on target, I remember thinking, "This is real." It seemed like there were a million thoughts racing through my mind, but that was the one that stood out above the rest. I brought my gun up on target and I started shooting. Because of the barricade, the only target I had was the right side of the subject's head. From the moment the situation escalated, I experienced a textbook example of tunnel vision. Everything around my target got kind of fuzzy and gray. It was like looking through a camera, where the center of the picture is sharply focused and everything around it is out of focus. I couldn't really see anything around me at all. I was entirely focused on my target. I knew that there was gunfire all around me, but it didn't matter. My only focus at that point was to hit my target. I knew that the subject was shooting and I had to stop him. All I could see was my front sight, and the subject's head recoiling as the bullets from my weapon struck him.

While I was shooting, another thought stood out in my mind as if at a higher volume than the rest of the thoughts racing through my head. I thought, "Is that enough?" Because the subject was sitting on the floor, leaning against the wall when the shooting started, in the chaos of the moment it was

v

difficult to tell when the subject no longer posed a threat. I lowered my weapon and looked at the subject. I had no idea how many times I had fired but it was obvious that the fight was over. I don't think it's possible to count the number of rounds fired under that kind of stress. I found out later that I had fired seven times. Six of the rounds had hit the subject in the side of the head and the seventh had struck him in the upper neck. He was dead.

The subject had fired three times, striking the lieutenant twice and his father once. My partner had fired six rounds and the lieutenant had fired eleven times. I remember hearing the shots during the whole thing but none of the shots seemed very loud, even though my partner's weapon was close to my right ear as he was shooting. My ear was ringing constantly for about three days after. Some of the shots fired by the lieutenant must have been fired after my partner and I had both stopped shooting, but I didn't hear them at all. In fact, at least one of the shots fired by the lieutenant was a contact shot that he fired after he was down. But I didn't hear it.

After I stopped shooting, it got very quiet in the room. It was a very eerie silence. Then I heard the lieutenant let out a moan. It was a sound that I'll never forget. Then, the next thing I remember is my partner yelling at me to take care of the lieutenant. I looked over and my partner was running out the door to call for help. I looked around the room and I didn't see anyone. I thought everyone but my partner and I had been shot. Then I realized that the sergeant was okay. He had been behind me during the shooting. In fact, he had drawn his weapon, and was preparing to shoot when I got in his line of fire. Luckily, he had the presence of mind to point his weapon down and he didn't fire. I holstered my weapon and ran to the lieutenant. I don't actually remember holstering my weapon, but I must have. It was holstered and snapped in.

In order to get into a position to be able to help the lieutenant, I had to straddle the subject that I had just shot. The lieutenant had ended up lying side by side with his assailant. The barricade was preventing me from approaching the lieutenant from the other side, so I climbed over the subject and tried to focus on the lieutenant. When I got to the lieutenant I asked him where he was hit and he told me he was shot in the chest. I took his gun and gave it to the sergeant, who was trying to take care of the father. I opened the lieutenant's shirt and I found a wound in his abdomen. He wasn't wearing body armor. I told him where the wound was and that I thought he would be okay. He wasn't responding. I couldn't even get him to make eye contact with me. He just kept looking straight up at the ceiling. I wanted to give him something to focus on so he wouldn't think about dying. My partner came back with a first aid kit and tossed me a couple of bandages. I placed one on the lieutenant's wound and I took another one and put it on his wrist. There was a piece of his wrist missing where one of the rounds had struck him. I grabbed his other hand and told him to hold the bandage in place. It wasn't bleeding much at all. I only did it to distract him. He held the bandage in place, but he was still not very responsive.

At one point the subject let out a death moan, and I looked over at him. He was already dead; his body was just reacting to the wounds. That was the first time I really looked at the subject after the shooting. The damage to his head was extensive and I remember feeling responsible for that damage. So I turned my attention back to the lieutenant.

It seemed like the paramedics got to the scene in seconds, but they actually arrived about six minutes after my partner called for help. The paramedics came in and took the lieutenant and the father away. Once they were gone, I had time to think about what had happened. The whole thing seemed very unreal. I didn't think at all about what I had to do. I just did it. It seemed completely automatic. Before this happened I had done a lot of mental rehearsal and I think that was one of the reasons it seemed so automatic.

Later, I was told that the first deputies who arrived were waving their hands to clear the smoke as they entered the room. I don't remember the smoke. Nor do I remember the shell casings that I was told were all over the floor when it was all over. I do remember the whole thing seeming almost dreamlike and the smoke in the air probably added to the effect.

I found out afterwards that the subject had his 9mm handgun loaded with a combination of ball ammo rounds and silver-tip hollow points. The first three rounds were ball ammo, and the rest of the magazine were alternating ball ammo and silver-tips. He also had spare magazines, which were fully loaded with ball ammo and silver-tips, alternating. Also, in his barricaded area were a mattress, a lamp, a telephone, and a small tape recorder.

When I look back at it, I never should have assumed that the gun was hidden just because the lieutenant didn't seem to be concerned. As it turned out, the subject had been holding the gun in his hand, in plain view, the entire time we were in the house. I couldn't see it because of the barricade, and the lieutenant gave absolutely no indication that we were in any danger. Trusting the lieutenant's tactics almost got me killed. An hour or so after the shooting, I found out that the lieutenant and the subject's father had both died. The lieutenant was one year away from retirement.

As survival instructors we believe that it is necessary to learn from each and every death of a fellow officer, so that we may hopefully prevent similar tragedies from occurring. Equally important, is the necessity to learn from the experiences of fellow officers who have faced the threat of death and survived. Additionally, it is not only the most violent of encounters that holds lessons to be learned. There is a great deal that we can learn from the day to day experiences of the law enforcement community. Throughout this book, you will find factual accounts of the experiences of many law enforcement officers. Each one is included to illustrate a specific point. While the names of the officers involved are not mentioned, their stories are told as related to the authors. While reading these accounts, keep in mind that although each story is intended to illustrate a particular point, many of the incidents discussed also contain examples of points covered elsewhere in this book. It is our hope that you can gain valuable insight from these incidents, and we suspect that you may be able to relate to some of the stories told, as you may have had similar experiences.

Chapter 1
Complacency

Think back to your earliest experiences on patrol. Chances are, if you really think about it, you will be able to see a definite difference in your attitude toward patrol back then. When you first entered the world of law enforcement you most likely expected the job to be somewhat dangerous, although you were probably a bit unsure as to the exact level of danger. So you were prepared, and eager, to handle anything. But then came the realities of patrol.

When you were dispatched to your first silent alarm call, you may have been expecting to catch a burglar breaking into a building. However, when you arrived at the call, you found that it was only a false alarm. Or perhaps a burglary had occurred, but the offenders were gone long before your arrival. Similarly, when you went to your first call of "shots fired in the area," you may have been expecting to confront an armed subject. Instead you patrolled the area for a time and found nothing. You may also have believed that no one would *want* to go to jail, and so you may have been expecting resistance during any and all arrests. However, you discovered that many times you received complete compliance.

There are many examples of situations that officers face every day that, more often than not, turn out to be much milder than they sounded when dispatched over the radio. Bar fights are often over and the combatants have already left the area when you arrive. When you arrive at the scene of a violent domestic dispute you find that the assailant has left the area. Shooting scenes and stabbing scenes are often occupied only by the victims and witnesses, with no offenders in sight. Building searches, more often than not, yield negative results. The list goes on and on.

After spending some time on patrol responding to these calls, you began to realize that many times the excitement is over before your arrival, and sometimes it's over even before anyone calls 911. Even when you were faced with violence or resistance, it was often nothing more than a mild physical altercation, which you were easily able to handle with your practiced skills, and possibly with backup. So as you went about your duties you found that the level of anxiety that you felt when being dispatched to a "hot" call was gradually decreasing as you gained experience on the job. This was due partially to the realization that most of the time you would not be in on the excitement of the call, and partially due to the experience that you had gained handling the excitement that you *did encounter.*

Although there are obvious benefits to gaining experience on the job, the downside here is that this is one of the causes of complacency. Responding to hundreds and hundreds of nonviolent calls takes its toll on your survival attitude. Imagine what it would be like if every call you responded to ended in a gunfight, or some other violent encounter. Your level of mental preparation would be extremely high. Your tactical and defensive skills would be finely honed. Every call dispatched would raise your anxiety level significantly. You would never go to a call expecting a false alarm. You would expect to face a life or death situation at every turn, and rightfully so. If, one day, you responded to a call that turned out to be nothing, you would be very pleasantly surprised. But this situation would present *less* danger than you anticipated instead of more.

In reality, however, you may make dangerous assumptions about the calls you are dispatched to. You may assume that each call, even one that may be very dangerous, is going to turn out to be nothing. Unfortunately, if this turns out to be a false assumption, you can find yourself in the middle of a fight for your life. The point is, of course, that you can't make assumptions about *any* call.

Sometimes officers make assumptions about calls based on similar calls that they have handled in the past. As you know, there are many similarities from call to call. Take domestic disputes, for example. The reasons for the arguments are often similar. There is almost invariably the involvement of alcohol or drugs. The level of violence is often similar. Many times the general area and time of day are no surprise either.

Traffic stops are another good example. In fact, traffic stops probably represent a greater complacency trap than domestic disputes, simply because they are probably a more frequent task for most officers, and they are *usually* uneventful. You stop a vehicle for a traffic violation, and in most cases, you write a citation or two and send the driver on his way. Just as with domestic disputes, there are many similarities from vehicle stop to vehicle stop. But there are always exceptions.

I was working as a patrol sergeant in one of the rural areas outside the city. One of the deputies I was supervising, an 8-year veteran of the department, stopped one of the local residents for not wearing his seatbelt. The deputy requested backup and I arrived to assist. The stop took place in front of the subject's residence and his wife stepped outside. The subject was uncooperative and belligerent, talking about weapons that he had inside the house. To make matters worse, he had a German Shepherd that was apparently trained to attack. In spite of all this, the deputy did not seem to sense any real danger. The subject decided that jail was a more reasonable choice then signing a citation, further increasing the level of danger. When we attempted to take him into custody, I trapped one of his hands and placed a handcuff on it. I thought the deputy would control the other hand, but the subject lashed out with a kick that the deputy was not ready for. As the subject pulled away, he ordered his German Shepherd to attack. The dog started to attack me and I immediately went for my gun, preparing to shoot the dog. Then the guy's wife got involved by getting between me and the dog, in an attempt to distract me. At this point the deputy was pinned up against his patrol car, with the subject punching him square in the face, ringing the tilt bell. I turned my attention back to the subject, and by using verbal commands, and drawing my side-handle baton, I was able to stop the attack on the deputy. Instead of getting a ticket, the guy went to jail on felony charges. When it was all over, I asked the deputy what he was thinking at the time of the stop regarding officer survival. All he could say was he really did not think the subject would punch him.

In addition to the dangers that law enforcement officers face from the people that they deal with on a daily basis, there is the risk of injury from motor vehicle accidents. This risk, while substantial, is often forgotten by the law enforcement community. This is another form of complacency that can create a dangerous situation for peace officers. Patrol officers spend a great deal of time behind the wheel and should be extremely alert to the dangers of the road. Every year law enforcement officers are accidentally killed in the line of duty. From 1989-1998, 493 lost their lives in automobile and motorcycle accidents and another 102 were struck and killed by vehicles while conducting traffic stops or directing traffic. (Law Enforcement Officers Killed and Assaulted 1998). The lesson here is obvious. You must be alert to the possibility of an accident. It seems that law enforcement officers tend to think of the danger related to police work only in terms of felonious assaults and the dangers posed by accidents are often brushed aside. It's important to remember that an accident can be just as deadly as an assault.

I was assigned to the graveyard shift as the relief sergeant and my squad was assigned to the north patrol area. Two of the deputies noticed a vehicle traveling at a high rate of speed. They attempted to stop the vehicle but the driver was not going to comply and a pursuit started. As our policy required, I was notified of all the factors, such as speed, traffic, and reason for the stop, and I allowed the pursuit to continue. I was a few blocks to the east and about a mile away, meeting with another one of the deputies, so we started into the area. As the pursuit continued, I found myself in a position parallel to the pursuit, with the other deputy behind me. The initial deputy advised they were turning onto a road and then onto a ditch bank that I knew would lead them right to us. I also knew that this area would be a bad location for a traffic stop, due to the location and known subjects in the neighborhood. As I approached the ditch bank, I realized I was going too fast to make the turn from pavement to loose gravel and dirt, so I stopped and turned my wheels to make the turn back to the ditch bank road. Prior to moving I checked behind me to insure I did not run into one of my own deputies and I realized the deputy behind me was not slowing down. He was coming straight at me and I was set up for a T-bone on the driver's side. I turned my wheels hard right and just about got the gas pushed when the deputy woke up and steered to the left. He took out the whole side of my unit, went through a fence, hit another car, pushing it into one more car before coming to rest. I felt lucky because we both walked away from the accident with minimal injuries but the property damage was extremely high. I knew the deputy was upset when he got out of his unit and he just kept saying over and over that crashing into his sergeant was not the best thing he could have done. When I asked him what happened, all he could say was he was not sure why he did not realize I was slowing down. He said, "I guess I must have fallen asleep."

Taking all of this into consideration, what can be done to combat complacency? First of all, you should never assume any outcome for any particular situation. The outcome of previous situations that you've handled has nothing to do with the outcome of the situation at hand. For example, never assume that the alarm call you are responding to will be a false alarm. Most officers have at least one chronic alarm in their patrol area, and they respond to it time and time again. The problem is that the alarm exists for a reason and can sound for a valid reason at any time. Obviously, if you assume that the alarm is false every time it goes off, your tactics when responding will suffer. As a result you may find yourself mentally unprepared to confront an intruder.

Or perhaps you are accustomed to finding the owner of the business at one of the chronic alarms in your patrol area. When you arrive, the door is open and you assume that it is the owner who has tripped the alarm in this case as well. But what if it's not? Will you be prepared if you are locked into the idea that it is the owner who tripped the alarm? Of course, it's good to be aware of the possibility that it may be the owner inside the building, otherwise, you may overreact to the situation. But to assume it is the owner and that you are in no danger could be a fatal error.

Additionally, you must never make assumptions about the people with whom you come into contact. People are not predictable and you cannot make assumptions about them based on size, gender, or prior contact. Law enforcement officers often remember individuals with whom they have had to fight during a call for service. The next time the officers encounter the subject they tend to be very cautious, even warning the other responding officers that the subject has been violent in the past so that they can be prepared as well. This is an excellent practice and should be continued. Even if the subject complies completely in all subsequent encounters, being prepared for the worst loses nothing. However, law enforcement officers also tend to judge nonviolent individuals that they encounter in the same manner. This is *not* a beneficial practice. There is no reason to believe that just because a subject has been compliant in the past, he will always be compliant.

Also, you must never assume that the initial information you receive will be accurate. Dispatchers may not receive accurate information from the caller. It's also possible that the dispatcher may make a mistake in relaying the information to you. Additionally, it takes time for the call to be received by the dispatcher and relayed to you. More time will pass before you actually arrive at the scene of the call. The circumstances of the scene can change even when the response time is minimal.

I was parked next to another officer and we were working on reports in the middle of the night shift. A guy drove up and told us that there was a domestic dispute across the street. He said that there was a man with a gun holding a woman hostage. He said they were inside the house and that the man would not let the woman leave. We drove down the street and approached the house slowly. It was completely dark as there were no streetlights in the area and the houses were set way back from the road. We got out on foot and began to approach the house. As I came around the corner of the house, I had my gun out in the low ready position with my flashlight off. That's where I made my mistake. The man who had reported the situation told us that the man with the gun was inside the house and because we got there so fast I assumed that he would still be inside. I was completely focused on the house and I didn't bother lighting up the yard as I approached. But then I heard a noise in front of the house and I lit up the area. There was a car in the yard with the door open and there was a guy sitting in the driver's seat with his legs out the door. He had his hands between his knees so I couldn't see if he was armed. I pointed my gun at him and ordered him to put his hands up. He just sat there looking at me. I kept yelling at him and he reached into the back seat with his left hand. When he brought his hands out again, they were empty. We grabbed him and cuffed him immediately. Afterwards, I looked in the back seat. There on the back seat where he had been reaching was a loaded, cocked and locked .45 caliber semiautomatic handgun. I don't know if he was reaching for it, or putting it down when I finally noticed him, but I guess it doesn't really matter. Either way, I screwed up. He could have shot me. I made the assumption that he would still be in the house and I was wrong. I won't make that mistake again.

Chapter 2
Command Presence

Command presence is your ability to portray authority by the way you present yourself on the scene of a call for service. You use it to control the scene without the need for stronger measures. It consists of everything from your appearance to your actions. Beginning with your appearance, you should be sure that you always present a professional appearance. Your uniform should be clean, pressed, and well maintained. Your boots and leather gear should be well maintained also. Tarnished brass and worn leather detract from a professional appearance.

Next, your choice of words should be professional as well. Obviously, in some situations it's necessary to be very forceful when talking to people, but this can be done in a professional manner, as well. In other words, compliance is usually best gained by being forceful and authoritative, without being insulting or derogatory. Everything you say can affect your situation. Your voice is a tool that you have at your disposal and should be thought of that way. By using it properly you can diffuse situations, calm people down, and you may even be able to resolve potentially violent situations peacefully. On the other hand, if you do not choose your words carefully, you may escalate a situation, making an arrest, or worse, necessary when it otherwise would not have been. Of course you know that some people and some situations will always require stronger measures in order to handle them effectively, but by carefully choosing your words you can help to insure that you are not the cause of the escalation of a situation.

I was working the night shift on patrol and we got a call of a domestic dispute at a residence nearby. I went to the call with another deputy. There were a man and a woman at the residence and they had both been drinking. The man had beaten up the woman and she had called 911. We separated them and I was talking to the woman. I asked her what had happened and she said, "He hit me." I asked her where he had hit her and she said, "Can't you tell? Look at me!" It was dark in the house, so I shined my flashlight on her face so

I could see her injuries. I looked at her face and I told her that her nose looked pretty bad and I thought it might be broken. She started yelling at me, telling me that he hadn't hit her in the nose. She said he had hit her in the eye and that there was nothing wrong with her nose. I looked again and I noticed that the area around her left eye was starting to swell. I guess her nose always looked like it had just been broken. I didn't know what to say after that. But it didn't matter because she was still yelling at me. It took me a good five minutes to get her calmed down so she would tell me the rest of her story.

Again, there are always people and circumstances that will require you to use physical force, but even in these situations it is possible to maintain a high degree of professionalism. For example, if a subject is resisting arrest, you must use the level of force necessary to effect the arrest, but no more. Then, once the subject is handcuffed and under control, the fight is over, which means you can again lower your level of force back to command presence with this particular subject. It will probably no longer be necessary to use a higher level of force unless the subject is continuing to fight, in spite of the restraints, which as you know, does occur from time to time. But if the subject stops resisting once the cuffs are in place, it can be very beneficial to lower your level of force to command presence. After all, you still have to deal with this subject during transportation and booking and you may obtain a higher level of compliance if you forget about the fight that just occurred. More importantly, if there are other subjects around during the arrest, you may be able to decrease the chances of any of them becoming involved in the fight if you maintain your professionalism. The more professional you are, the more likely it is that they will see you as "just doing your job" rather than as harassing one of their own. As a result, they may choose to stay out of your way. Obviously, there are many factors that determine the level of involvement of bystanders and others at a call for service, and there is no guarantee that professionalism will keep you safe, but it is one factor that can work in your favor. You have most likely developed a certain level of command presence during your years of experience and you have probably noticed from time to time how valuable it can be.

I was working the graveyard shift and I stopped a vehicle that didn't have any taillights. The driver pulled into a commercial area where he worked and got out of the truck. He went to the door and was trying to get his key in the lock, but he was too drunk to get the door open. I told him to put the keys down but he ignored me. I finally got the keys away from him and got his driver's license. I told him I was going to administer field sobriety tests and he refused to cooperate. I checked his license and found a warrant. There was no backup available so I knew I was on my own. The guy was about six inches taller than me and outweighed me by at least 75 pounds. He was leaning against the side of the truck and I told him he was under arrest and I ordered him to turn around and put his hands behind his back. He stood up straight, puffed out his chest, and looked me up and down slowly. I knew what he was doing. He was sizing me up and trying to decide if he should comply or fight. I figured he would choose to fight so I started formulating a plan to take him down fast, because this guy was big and I didn't want to fight him. Then he turned around and put his hands behind his back. I cuffed him in a heartbeat. After he was cuffed, he decided he wanted to fight.

It's important to remember that people can, and will, assess a peace officer's abilities based on the officer's command presence, or lack thereof. In the following example, the subject even explains how he did this.

I was a field sergeant working the graveyard shift. Calls for service had been slow for most of the shift until one of the officers under my command called out a traffic stop. I was several miles away and started into the area in case he needed backup. After about a minute the officer got back on the air and called out a pursuit. Given the time of day and the traffic conditions, I allowed the pursuit to go on. At this point we were not sure why the subject decided to run after he had already stopped his vehicle and had even had contact with the officer. The pursuit took us around the patrol area several times and the subject made several attempts to run the patrol cars off the road. The subject was finally stopped and the officers safely took him into custody. When things had calmed down, I asked the guy why he ran and to my surprise he was brutally honest. He said, "My girlfriend is getting ready to leave town and I just had to see her one more time. I'm in a hurry, and yeah, I was speeding when the officer stopped me. But the officer looked like such a goof I figured if I took off he wouldn't know what to do and I would get away." I spent a little more time with the subject and found out what he meant when he said the officer looked like a "goof." He explained that the officer looked unkempt in his uniform and personal appearance, and he said that the officer did not sound confident when he spoke. Based on his assessment of the officer, he decided to run. He could have decided to attack the officer.

A law enforcement officer's level of command presence can even play a part in a subject's decision to attempt to kill the officer. Officers have been killed because they were perceived as careless or unprepared by their assailants. According to studies published in Killed in the Line of Duty, it was not uncommon for offenders who killed law enforcement officers to evaluate the officers prior to committing to an assault. In one such case study an offender who had set out to kill an officer aborted an attack on the first officer he encountered after evaluating that officer. He then launched a successful attack on the next officer that he encountered after deciding that the second officer would be an easy target.

One subject involved in a similar case study, also published in Killed in the Line of Duty, stated that the officer that he killed *"was not authoritarian and did not take control of me. He was a willing participant in his death."* Other offenders stated that they felt that if the slain officers had been more "professional" they would not have been killed. Based on this information, it is very difficult to discount the importance of command presence.

Chapter 3
Muscle Memory

Muscle memory is your body's natural tendency to learn movements that are repeated frequently and then repeat them when necessary without conscious thought. For example, if you carry your wallet in the same pocket every day, you do not have to think about where it is when you need it. You reach for it automatically. If you change its location, the first time you need it you will find yourself reaching for it in its old location. Muscle memory is something you have undoubtedly experienced during your daily activities and there are plenty of examples in law enforcement. When you started out on patrol, you probably spent a fair amount of time setting up your patrol car so that everything was within easy reach. You probably also took great care in positioning the equipment on your duty belt. You positioned everything in your car and on your belt so that it would be easily accessible when needed. You knew that there would be times when you would need a piece of equipment and you would not have time to waste in retrieving it. So you were careful in the organization of your equipment.

You've probably noticed since then that you've become very accustomed to the location of each and every piece of equipment that you carry. When you need your handcuffs, for example, you don't have to think about where they are. You reach for them automatically because they're always in the same spot. This is muscle memory and it happens because you've carried your handcuffs in the same location and reached for them in that location time after time after time.

Now what happens if you change the location of your handcuffs? In your years of experience you may have had occasion to rearrange your equipment a time or two. Maybe you were issued a new piece of equipment that made it necessary to reorganize. Or perhaps you changed assignments and found yourself in plainclothes instead of in uniform. Whatever the reason, when you changed the position of your handcuffs on your belt, the next time you needed them you found yourself reaching for them in their old location. It took some time for you to get used to their new position.

You've probably changed vehicles from time to time as well. When your patrol car is replaced, you find yourself driving a newer model, or perhaps even one made by a different manufacturer. Your new car is designed differently and may require a different organizational structure. You may be able to keep your equipment in locations similar to those in your old vehicle but you may not. The greater the change, the more difficult the adjustment.

This is not to say that these adjustments can't be made, but they take time. Therefore, whenever it becomes necessary to make a change, you must be aware of the effect on your muscle memory, and the time it will take for you to become accustomed to the new location of your equipment.

Additionally, because of muscle memory, you should never make changes simply for the sake of change. The location of each piece of equipment that you may need when under stress should be carefully thought out. Then, once positioned in your car or on your belt, each piece of equipment should be left in that location unless it becomes absolutely necessary to move it. For example, you should never switch from a belt holster to a shoulder holster simply for convenience or style. You may have been drawing your weapon from a belt holster for years. Switching to a shoulder holster could take hundreds of repetitions to fully re-train your muscle memory. If a change is *necessary*, make the change, and practice, practice, practice. If the change is not necessary, stick to your belt holster.

When you're reaching for your wallet and muscle memory comes into play, it won't be a major catastrophe if your muscle memory is not fully trained. On the other hand, if you're going for your handgun while under fire, muscle memory is critical. The sudden stress of a gunfight can make it very difficult to focus on something that should be deeply ingrained, such as the location of your firearm. Think about it. When you are faced with a situation requiring an immediate deadly force response, your reactions must be instantaneous. You will not have time to adjust your drawing technique from one holster location to another. Not only will you not have the time, but also you may not have the presence of mind. You may be so intently focused on the threat that you may, at least briefly, be unaware that you're attempting to draw your weapon from the wrong location. Then, when you become aware that you are trying to draw your weapon from its old location, you have to take another moment to think about its new location, and then correct your actions.

The disadvantages here are twofold. First, attempting to draw your weapon from the wrong location wastes valuable time. Correcting your draw wastes even more time. Obviously, it would be much faster to draw your weapon instantly when it's needed. Because law enforcement officers are almost always behind the power curve to start with, you can't afford to waste even one split-second.

Second, in order to correct your mistake, you have to think consciously about what you're doing. When you're in this situation, you will have a lot to think about. You will be faced with the threat of death, or great bodily harm. You will have tactical decisions to make. There will be lives at stake, possibly innocent civilian lives in addition to your own life. You won't need the added distraction of a muscle memory problem.

You should make every effort to stick to one practical location for each piece of equipment that you carry, not just your sidearm. Under stress, you don't need to be thinking about where you are carrying your weapon, or your handcuffs, or anything else, for that matter. You may have much more important things to focus on, such as survival.

Muscle memory may be one of the most important things you accomplish in this profession in terms of your survival. Almost every aspect of your daily life revolves around some type of muscle memory. The phone rings and you just simply pick it up, the radio dispatcher calls your number and you grab the mic and respond, and the list goes on and on. You can see that muscle memory is not only related to physical movements but it is also linked to the mental thought process as well. As you train the response of your muscle groups, you train the brain to remember the action. You can continue to train responses mentally without actually involving physical movements by using mental rehearsal and mental practice.

Chapter 4
Sudden Stress Syndrome

Y ou have probably considered the possibility that when you find yourself facing a life or death situation, your skills and your perception may be affected in some way. Sudden Stress Syndrome includes the physiological changes that occur as a result of sudden and extreme stress, as well as the effects that these changes can have on your perception and your motor skills performance. These changes can have both negative and positive effects in a survival situation. The key to keeping your chances of survival as high as possible is to understand the ways you may be affected and how to avoid or counteract the negative effects.

Physiological Effects of Sudden Stress Syndrome

First, you should know that under stress there are certain physiological changes that your body goes through. When a situation is interpreted by the brain as threatening, the pituitary gland releases the hormone ACTH (Adrenocorticotropic hormone), which causes the adrenal gland to release the hormone cortisol into the bloodstream. These hormones act on cells throughout the body. When you combine the effects of the adrenal hormones with the activation of the sympathetic nervous system, you end up with the fight or flight syndrome. As you may remember, fight or flight is the instinctive urge to run (flight) or stand your ground and fight. When you receive training and reinforce it with practice you will have more than an instinctive reaction to this stress. Your training will tell you whether to tactically retreat or stand your ground and finish the fight.

Additionally, there are other physiological changes that occur under high stress. Your breathing becomes deeper and the bronchi in the lungs become dilated to take in more oxygen. Your spleen contracts, releasing stored red blood cells to carry this additional oxygen. Your heart rate increases in order to pump oxygen more rapidly through your system. Your liver releases stored sugar for use by your muscles. Your blood is redistributed from the skin and the viscera, to the muscles and the brain. Your pupils become dilated. There is an increase in the special blood cells known as lymphocytes, which help to repair damaged tissues, as well as an increase in the blood's ability to coagulate. All of these changes occur in a matter of minutes or even seconds.

Effects of Sudden Stress Syndrome on Motor Skills

There have been many studies over the years regarding the relationship between stress and motor skill performance. This research is the basis for the Inverted-U Hypothesis. The Inverted-U Hypothesis, simply put, states that as your stress level increases, your motor skills performance improves, but only up to a point, after which your motor skill performance will deteriorate with additional increases in stress. According to the Inverted-U Hypothesis, fine motor skills, such as those involving the hands and fingers, can deteriorate at around 115 beats per minute (BPM). This is followed by the deterioration of complex motor skills, involving multiple muscle groups, at about 145 BPM. Gross motor skills, involving large muscle groups, which require very little decision making, however, actually reach optimal levels of performance during high stress. In Sharpening The Warrior's Edge, Bruce Siddle wrote, "The research clearly indicates that fine and complex motor skills begin to deteriorate when the working heart rate accelerates beyond 145 beats per minute." Siddle also wrote, "at 115 beats per minute (BPM) fine motor skills (precision and accuracy skills) deteriorate. When the heart rate exceeds 145 BPM, complex motor skills deteriorate."

It's important to understand that by the time the heart rate reaches 145 BPM, both fine and complex motor skills are deteriorating. Therefore, survival skills should incorporate gross motor skills whenever possible. "Since it is reasonable to expect any survival situation to increase the student's heart rate beyond 145 beats per minute, all survival training should be based on gross motor skills whenever possible." (Siddle, 1995)

To complicate matters, survival situations often require motor skills to be utilized not only with maximum proficiency, but with maximum speed as well. Wasted time can mean the difference between life and death. Your reactions in a high stress situation must be immediate to ensure the best chances for survival. If you get behind the power curve, catching up can be difficult, at best. In violent encounters peace officers often start out behind the power curve, simply due to the fact that they are most often reacting to the actions of an assailant. This is not to say that overcoming this disadvantage is impossible, for it certainly is not. If it were, there would be many more law enforcement officers killed in the line of duty. However, it remains true that action is faster than reaction and that puts you at a serious disadvantage. When your life is suddenly in grave danger because of someone else, you will be responding to his or her actions. This causes an inherent delay, which can cause your stress level to escalate immediately as you realize that not only are you in extreme danger, but your attacker has the advantage, in terms of speed.

One of the best ways to combat this is to remain alert and ready for an attack if it comes. Many officers involved in life or death encounters have stated that they initially felt surprise when attacked. This is common, but can be costly. When faced with sudden violence, your response must be instantaneous. Thoughts of surprise can slow your response time. On the other hand, if you are mentally prepared for an attack, you will waste no time in your response. It will be immediate, increasing your survival odds.

Obviously, another way to combat the fact that you will most likely be reacting to the actions of your assailant is to be well practiced in your survival skills. For example, drawing your sidearm should be second nature, so that when it is needed, it can be drawn smoothly and quickly. The more practiced your skills are, and the better prepared you are mentally for a violent confrontation, the greater your chances for survival if you should find yourself starting off behind the power curve.

Effects of Sudden Stress Syndrome on Perception

You may have heard the terms "Perceptual Distortions," (Artwohl, Christensen, 1997) or "Tache Psyche Effect." These terms were derived from numerous studies dealing with the physical and psychological effects of sudden stress. Even if you haven't heard these specific terms, you might recognize the symptoms from past experiences or past training. With this in mind let's look at some perceptual distortions that can occur during Sudden Stress Syndrome.

Auditory Exclusion / Diminished Sound

If you experience this, sounds may be diminished or muffled, or you may not hear some sounds at all. The sound of gunfire, shouting, or any other noise, which would normally be very loud, can be affected. It is important to be aware of this in the event of a sudden stress situation. If you experience auditory exclusion or diminished sound you may not hear important danger cues, or you may not hear other officers on the scene attempting to communicate things such as tactical plans, or the location of suspects. You must also be aware of the possibility of auditory exclusion or diminished sound in the event that another officer on the scene experiences it. You may find yourself shouting at another officer in an attempt to warn him of danger or communicate your intentions, and you may get no response. Be prepared for the fact that auditory exclusion or diminished sound can affect any officer on the scene.

Intensified Sounds

It's also possible that some sounds may seem much louder than normal. For example, you may hear the cylinder of a weapon turn and lock into its firing position. You may experience this as well as auditory exclusion or diminished sound during the same event.

Tunnel Vision

When you experience tunnel vision, your vision becomes intensely focused on the perceived threat and your peripheral vision is reduced or eliminated. Tunnel vision is very much like it sounds. It may appear as if you are looking at the threat through a cylinder. The area in the center, or the threat, may appear to be exceptionally well focused, while the area around it may appear to be hazy, gray, or even black. Something to consider is that if you get tunnel vision when faced with a gun and you make the decision to shoot, you may not place your shots as accurately as you would otherwise. If you tunnel in on the gun, your shots will probably be directed at the gun. It's common for arms, hands, and guns to be shot during gunfights, because officers and their assailants are both susceptible to tunnel vision.

Heightened Visual Clarity

You may see some things with extraordinary clarity or detail. You may experience this by itself or, as mentioned above, in conjunction with tunnel vision.

Automatic Pilot

You may experience the sensation of responding to the threat giving little, or no, conscious thought to your actions. This is where your training takes over. You may remember hearing during your academy training that under stress you will revert to training. This is exactly what your academy instructors were talking about. When you are faced with the threat of death or great bodily harm, you will respond the way you have been trained. It will happen very fast, and without the need for conscious decision making, causing it to feel completely automatic. You may even experience the feeling that you were not in control at that moment. In reality, however, you were in control, and you were responding appropriately to the threat.

Distortion of Time and Events

You may experience the sensation of Slow Motion Time, in which everything seems to be taking longer to happen than it normally would. Officers who experience this sometimes report a greater level of confidence than expected during the event. Because of the fact that things seemed to slow down considerably, they felt that they had plenty of time to respond to the threat to ensure their safety. Conversely, you may experience Fast Motion Time in which everything appears to be happening much faster than normal.

Memory Related Distortions

Your memory of the event may be affected in a number of ways. You may recall something from the event that did not actually occur. This can include something you saw, or heard, or it could be your actions or the actions of someone else involved in the event. In fact, it can be related to anything you may experience during a critical incident. Or you may not remember parts of the event that actually occurred. This can include the inability to remember some of your own actions.

Disassociation

You may experience the sensation that you are detached from the event, as if you were dreaming, or as if you were looking at yourself from outside your body.

Intrusive Distracting Thoughts

During the incident you may experience thoughts not directly relevant to the immediate situation. This could include such things as thinking about family or friends, or what you plan to do after work, etc.

Temporary Paralysis

You may experience the sensation of feeling temporarily paralyzed and unable to move.

It's important to understand that incidents do not have to involve gunfire to bring about the effects of Sudden Stress Syndrome.

I was dispatched to a domestic dispute with another officer. It was a typical domestic. The woman had been beaten up, the kids were crying, and the offender was drunk. He was in the back bedroom, and he started yelling and screaming as soon as we got there. We were in the back bedroom with him and he was going crazy. We were standing next to the dresser and he was about three feet away. The top of the dresser was cluttered with all kinds of junk. Suddenly he got quiet and his eyes moved to the top of the dresser. I followed his eyes down to the dresser to see what he was looking at. Right away I found what he was looking at. There was a large kitchen knife lying on top of the dresser. As soon as I saw the knife everything slowed down and I was looking at the knife through a little tunnel. Then this hand entered the tunnel that I was looking at the knife through and it was so slow. It seemed like it took an eternity and then his hand got to the handle of the knife at the same time that my hand got to his. At that point I grabbed his hand, everything sped up again, and I did a wrist roll, breaking his hand, and took him to the ground.

In the following incident a sergeant describes how he experienced auditory exclusion, automatic pilot, distortion of time and events, and intrusive, distracting thoughts.

I was doing a background investigation on an applicant who worked for another law enforcement agency 30 miles outside of my jurisdiction. At the end of my interview with a co-worker and his sergeant, the sergeant and I were outside of the station talking. An individual walked up to us and by the actions of the local sergeant I did not perceive this subject as a threat even though he was carrying a six-foot piece of metal conduit. This quickly changed as he started to give us a hard time. He struck the sergeant square on the chin with his closed fist. The sergeant was knocked out instantly and as he hit the ground I heard a loud, hollow thump from his head. At this point I was unsure if he was even alive and can remember thinking to myself "I have never seen anyone hit that hard in my life." The two people who were waiting for me to leave so they could go to coffee with the sergeant left and I never even heard them start their truck or drive off. Now the subject was holding the pipe in a baseball bat type hold and was looking toward me. Without thinking I drew my sidearm and started to give verbal commands to the subject to drop the weapon. The guy stepped toward me and I took a step back giving commands to drop the weapon. He took another step at which point I told the subject that if he did not drop the weapon or if he took another step I would shoot him. He dropped the weapon and I ordered him to the ground but he did not comply. At this point I thought about creating distance, but I was concerned about the sergeant, who besides being injured, presented an additional safety issue because his weapon was accessible to the suspect. I thought about my walkie-talkie only to realize I was too far away from dispatch to communicate. Ironically, I was just outside of the sergeant's police station. I could even see the radio room. The door was open but the operator's terminal was on the wrong side of it and the dispatcher could not see me. I turned my thoughts to lowering my force options to the side-handle baton. I had two side handle batons but they were both locked inside my unit. As I attempted to open the door, the subject advanced and then stopped again as I turned my attention back to him. We did this several more times before I decided this wasn't going to work. I turned my attention back to the sergeant for just a second and I couldn't tell if he was breathing, but he was still not moving. It seemed as if ten minutes had passed while I was trying to get this subject to comply, and trying to come up with a plan to take him down. Finally, one of the local officers arrived, and to my surprise the subject turned his attention to the local. He then went after the local officer with the pipe. Next, a firefighter/paramedic arrived and I assumed he would take care of the sergeant so I helped cover the local officer. We both had our guns drawn because of the pipe, but every time I moved in an attempt to remove the crossfire situation the suspect moved, too. Two additional officers arrived on scene and we were able to get the subject contained far enough away from the sergeant for the paramedics to do their thing, but they stayed back. I asked them why they weren't attending to the sergeant and they told me that as long as the subject was not in custody they would not turn their backs on him. That was when I found out that everyone on the scene, except me, knew the subject. The subject finally surrendered, and I got a chance to see the applicant in action, but the sergeant was seriously injured. He survived, but when his head hit the ground he received substantial damage to his brain which left him like a child and ended his career in law enforcement.

Here's an excellent example of visual and memory related distortions.

I had a reserve officer riding with me one night and we were dispatched to a 911 call. What we didn't know was that the person who had called 911 had been shot in the back of the head and killed by his brother while he was on the phone. The shooter had also shot his own mother. When we arrived in the area with the other unit that was my backup, we unknowingly pulled up in front of the residence. I saw a subject step out of the house across the street from me and he immediately started shooting at us with a semiautomatic rifle. I bailed out and as I was running around the back of the car for cover the bullets were hitting the patrol car behind me. How I didn't

The Officer Survival Creed

The will to survive, to survive the attack, must be uppermost in my mind. For the one who lives through a fight is better off than the one who does not. Therefore, preparation and not paranoia is the key to my survival. To survive I must be aware, be alert, be confident, be deceptive, be decisive, and be ready. I must expect the unexpected and do the unexpected.

When faced with violent assault, my life depends upon my reaction without hesitation. There is no time to ponder because to ponder is to possibly perish. My response, if attacked, must not be fear but aggressiveness. I must block out all thoughts of my own peril and think only of stopping the assailant.

My prize in personal defense is my life. The perfect fight is one that is over before the loser realizes what is happening. The perfect defense is a counterattack that succeeds before the enemy can attack again. Therefore, if I am assaulted, I will retaliate instantly. I will be sudden and quick. I will be fast, not fair. Speed is my salvation.

If my attacker knocks me down, I will fight back against the odds and get up off the ground. I will seize the initiative and take every advantage. My concern is to stay alive. I won't hold back.

If I find myself under lethal attack, I won't be kind. I will be harsh and tough. If I must shoot, I will shoot with precision and shoot to stop. If I must use my hands, I will use them with all the strength I possess and more. When I strike, I will strike hard; I will kick, punch, and do what must be done to survive. I will strike no more after my attacker is incapable of further action, but I will see that he is stopped.

Above all, I won't give up and I will make it. I will not die in the streets, or in an alley, or in any other part of the concrete jungle. I will survive; not just by good luck and good fortune, but by my skills.

If I adhere to these basic principles of survival and adhere to the attitude that is suggested in them, as a police officer, I will greatly enhance and perfect my skills in utilizing good and safe practices, tactics, and techniques.

Peter M. Lopez, LAPD

get hit, I'll never know. We took cover behind the car and he kept us pinned down for quite a while. There was a street light behind us and whenever we looked over the unit to get a shot at the guy he would start shooting again and we'd have to get back down behind the patrol car. Eventually, help arrived and another deputy shot the subject with a rifle, killing him. Afterward, I told the detectives that the subject was wearing green camouflage fatigues, and that he had bandoleros across his chest with extra ammo in them. To this day I can still see him standing at the front door dressed as I described. He looked just like a character from a war movie. But the detectives told me that he was actually wearing blue jeans and a white T-shirt. They also asked me how my flashlight got all the way up onto the front porch near the subject. I didn't know. Apparently, I had thrown it at him during the shooting and I had absolutely no memory of it. I still don't remember throwing it.

In the following example, a deputy experiences several effects of Sudden Stress Syndrome.

I was working swing shift in the summer and it was hot at the beginning of the shift, so I decided to stop at the drive-up for a cold drink. As I got to the intersection near the drive-up I noticed an officer from another department standing behind his patrol unit, which was parked next to the sidewalk. When I arrived at the intersection, I noticed the officer point and fire his handgun several times at an armed man that was walking backwards facing the officer. As I reached for my mic, I noticed that the officer was having some kind of problem with his firearm. I advised radio of the situation by saying "S.O., P.D.'s in a shoot-out on the bridge." I didn't believe what I was seeing. Someone was shooting at an officer. I then blocked traffic with my patrol car. As I exited my vehicle, I could hear the dispatcher requesting more information from me but I was unable to respond because I had to help the officer. As I ran toward cover, I yelled at the bystanders to clear the area. As I reached cover behind a vehicle, I looked toward the suspect. I noticed that he had his hands down at his side and was walking away from the officer. Then the suspect turned toward the officer and pointed a small handgun at him. The suspect fired his weapon at the officer and I thought he fired two rounds. I wasn't sure because I didn't hear what I was expecting, the rounds sounded like firecrackers. I fired one round at the suspect. Not knowing if I had hit the suspect I moved to the rear of the vehicle to get a clearer shot. As I approached this position, I couldn't hear any gunfire from the officer. I thought either he was hit or he was unable to fix his weapon malfunction. I then thought that the suspect might have been hit because he laid down on the sidewalk. The suspect, while lying down, pointed his weapon at the officer again and I fired two more rounds. At this point the suspect stopped moving. I approached the suspect and I noticed that he still had the firearm at his side. I retreated to my original position of cover for a few moments while I assessed the scene. I did not know at this point if the officer was O.K. or if the suspect was injured. Unlike on TV the suspect did not get thrown backwards and scream and holler in pain. I didn't see blood flying or body parts being torn apart from the body. Although the responding units from the other agency were responding code three, I never heard the sirens. I also had tunnel vision at this point as I was intently focused on the suspect. From the second round I fired, time seemed to slow down and I felt like it took forever for backup units to arrive. When the first backup officer from the other agency arrived, without speaking we approached the suspect. When another one of the city officers had arrived on the scene, we secured the suspect by handcuffing him and securing the firearm. Once the incident was over and other officers arrived on a scene I was approached by the initial officer involved in the shooting and he thanked me for helping him. He said that he had two weapon malfunctions during the shooting. The suspect was struck by two of my rounds. One penetrated his upper midsection and traveled through his body and the second struck his hand and damaged his firearm. I was twenty feet away from the suspect at the time of the shooting.

Some of the effects of Sudden Stress Syndrome can be overcome, or at least minimized, to a certain degree with the use of muscle memory. For example, if you get tunnel vision and auditory exclusion in a sudden stress situation, you may be able to clear up both of these symptoms if you physically move your head from left to right when there is a lull in the action. If you practice this at the live fire range after each stage of fire you will continue to build or reinforce this part of your muscle memory.

Some effects of Sudden Stress Syndrome can be minimized by deep breathing exercises. You know that under sudden stress your motor skills can be affected due to the increase in your heart rate. By breathing in deeply and slowly, holding the breath for a moment, and exhaling slowly you can lower your heart rate and improve the efficiency of your fine and complex motor skills under stress.

Simply being aware of them and being prepared for them before they happen to you can combat other effects of Sudden Stress Syndrome. For example, if you experience auditory exclusion, and you are prepared for it, you may be aware of the fact that you could be missing important danger cues. Even if the awareness of auditory exclusion does not stop the effect, by being aware of it you can compensate by looking around for other assailants, for example.

Chapter 5

Mental Rehearsal and Mental Practice

Mental rehearsal can be a valuable tool in preparing you for a life-threatening encounter. Mental rehearsal has been around since as early as the 1940's, and Dr. Joseph Jastrow first studied the link between the mental process and physical skills in 1892. Professional athletes have been using the idea for years, visualizing themselves successfully competing before the event begins. In The Nature and Conditions of Learning, Howard L. Kingsley wrote, "the development of skill requires physical practice on the part of the learner, although mental practice can assist the process."

As a practical example, recall the last time you flew a commercial airline. At the beginning of each flight is a safety briefing for the benefit of all on board. You may have noticed that during the briefing many passengers seemed uninterested and paid no attention. Perhaps they have flown often enough to become comfortable with the emergency procedures, or perhaps they are simply not worried about the possibility of an emergency landing, or a crash. You may have also noticed that other passengers paid close attention and some may have even reviewed the safety literature provided in the seat pocket. They may have been new to commercial air travel, or possibly they were just safety conscious.

Now suppose your flight had experienced some type of mechanical failure, resulting in a survivable crash. All other factors being equal, who do you think would have the best chance for survival? Would it be the first-time flyer who ignored the safety briefing, or would it be the first-time flyer who paid close attention, and perhaps even went so far as to review the safety literature and take a look around to be sure of the location of the nearest exit?

Obviously, the one who paid attention and knows what to do is ahead of the game here. But what about the experienced flyer who did not listen to the briefing simply because he has heard it over and over again in his travels? Where does he fit into all this? He is probably better off than the first-time flyer who paid no attention at all because he at least has some idea of what he should do. However, he's probably not as prepared as the well-prepared first-time flyer because he hasn't paid attention *recently*, or taken the time to learn the location of the nearest exits on this particular flight. It is doubtful that all of his flying is done on the same model or size of aircraft, and equally doubtful that he occupies the same seat on every flight. Therefore, it would be beneficial to listen to the safety briefing and check for the location of the closest exit on each and every flight. In the event of an emergency, there will be no time wasted in looking for the nearest exit. Every precious second will be used as efficiently as possible by taking the necessary action to ensure survival.

This is one of the main benefits of mental rehearsal. When the time comes to make life or death decisions, mental rehearsal prepares you by speeding up the process. It is easier to make the right decisions when you have practiced beforehand. Imagine spending even one second looking for the emergency exit in the wreckage of a commercial airliner. It would be much easier, and faster, if you already knew which direction to go. Yes, locating the exit may only take a moment, but that moment could mean the difference between life and death. On the other hand, finding the exit in the heat of the moment may be much more difficult than you expected. There will be commotion and possibly panic. There may be smoke and fire to contend with. Additionally, you may have to find your way out in total darkness. You can prepare yourself for any emergency situation that occurs on duty or off duty, by using mental rehearsal.

Mental rehearsal should include things that you may not have thought about before. It should incorporate situations that cannot be included in training and practice sessions for reasons of safety or practicality. For example, imagine being involved in a shooting where it becomes necessary for you to shoot through a window. Suppose you are conducting a daytime vehicle stop that goes bad. In this particular scenario you are using a passenger side approach and you end up exchanging gunfire with the driver of the vehicle through a closed window. Regardless of who fires first, once the window has been broken, it will shatter across its entire surface. That's what safety glass used in vehicles is designed to do. The windows of this particular vehicle are lightly tinted which keeps the glass from collapsing as a result of the impact of the bullets passing through it. As a result, you will no longer be able to see your assailant. Of course it can be difficult to see through windows that are even lightly tinted, but it becomes even more difficult when the window is shattered. Your assailant's movements and condition will be more difficult to ascertain. Did you stop the threat? Is your attacker capable of continuing the assault? Has he changed positions to get a better shot at you, or make better use of cover? Is he still in the vehicle? Are there other threats in the vehicle that bear watching?

All these questions have just become a little more difficult to answer now that you have one less window to look through. Of course, there are other windows on the vehicle you can use and it will only take a second or two to adjust your plan and get into a position of advantage. You may move quickly into a position where you can see into the vehicle through a different window, or you may drop back into a position that allows you to see the entire vehicle and stay behind cover while issuing verbal commands to the assailant. Whatever you decide to do, you will need to alter your tactical plan. You can't afford to stay in a position of disadvantage.

Obviously, this is only one scenario, and your chances of being involved in an actual incident that is just like it may not be very high, but you could find yourself in a similar situation. Remember that vehicles are not the only places where you will find tinted glass. The idea is to think about these things ahead of time so that you aren't taken by surprise by the sudden loss of visual contact with your attacker. By using mental rehearsal, you can formulate tactical plans ahead of time and come up with different options to use in a variety of situations. Remember that the options you come up with are only options and none should be considered an absolute solution. You will have to decide which option to exercise if you are ever faced with this situation in reality. Mental rehearsal can help you to make this decision quickly and effectively, by giving you "experience." When you find yourself faced with a life or death decision, you may be forced to make split-second decisions for the first time under extreme stress, but it won't be the first time you've made those decisions.

Obviously you can't predict the future, and even if you do extensive mental rehearsal, chances are probably slim that when you do become involved in a critical incident it will bear a significant resemblance to your practiced incidents. Even if the real life incident is similar in nature to a scenario you have rehearsed, there are bound to be handfuls of differences. This doesn't mean that mental rehearsal won't be effective. The "experience" you gain in mental rehearsal can help you in any situation.

In your experience driving you have undoubtedly had a few close calls and each one was unique. Additionally, the way in which you avoided a collision in each situation was probably unique in some way. The fact that each experience is unique in no way negates the positive effects of the experience. Each narrowly avoided collision can better prepare you for the next time.

Additionally, you can use mental rehearsal to practice and prepare for situations that may unfold in real life in a way that very much resembles your imagination. For example, imagine encountering a knife-wielding subject in the middle of a dark street. You can surely imagine the lighting and other surrounding environment if you are creating this scenario in an area that you normally patrol. If you also imagine that the subject is someone with whom you have frequent contact, your scenario will be much more realistic. Now imagine your assailant moving toward you aggressively and attempting to stab you. Next, imagine your tactics as you neutralize the threat. Then do it again and change it up a little. Maybe this time the subject's distance from you is different. Or maybe the knife is being held in a different position, or in the opposite hand. Perhaps you can change the surrounding conditions, such as the position or number of bystanders, for example.

In this exercise you have combined many of the most important elements of mental rehearsal. You are practicing a situation that cannot be easily practiced without the benefit of mental rehearsal. You are also creating your scenario using familiar elements, which can greatly enhance the realism of the exercise. Last, but certainly not least, you are repeating the exercise and incorporating changes into it as you do so. This helps you to prepare for a variety of situations by allowing you to practice a variety of responses under different circumstances.

Creating scenarios in mental rehearsal that are as realistic as possible is one of the keys to using mental rehearsal effectively. In Deadly Force Encounters, Artwohl and Christensen recommend that you make the mental image as complete as possible in order to ensure the highest level of realism attainable. This means creating scenarios that even include sounds and smells. "If you make it vivid enough in your mind, you may even experience a sense of nervousness and an accelerated heart rate." (Artwohl, Christensen, 1997) Artwohl and Christensen also recommend that your scenario should not take any longer to complete in your mind than it would in reality. This, too, adds to the level of realism in your mental rehearsal. As you know, realistic training and practice can be extremely beneficial.

Perhaps the most important component in mental rehearsal is to always visualize yourself winning at the end of each scenario you create. You should never visualize yourself being killed by the suspect or suspects. To do so would be detrimental to your survival attitude. It can be beneficial, however, to imagine yourself getting injured, and continuing to get the job done, in your scenario. Part of mental rehearsal is training yourself never to give up, even if you are shot, or stabbed, or injured in some other way. So it may help you to develop this mindset if you imagine that you could become injured, and then imagine yourself fighting through the pain and coming out of the situation victorious. Do not, however, imagine that your injury in your scenario is the result of a tactical error on your part. This would also be self-defeating. In fact, the majority of the scenarios that you play out when mentally rehearsing should not include any injuries to you at all. Scenarios in which you are injured should only be rehearsed occasionally, in order to reinforce your belief that you can survive under any circumstances.

It's important to remember that when you rehearse a scenario where you are injured, a proper mental attitude must be practiced. If you think you will die if you get shot, that is exactly what might happen. There have been horror stories told about people who have died from non-lethal gunshot wounds. There is no scientific reason for it but it still happens, and perhaps even more remarkable are the cases where lethal wounds are sustained and the subject survives. This may be due to the subject's attitude toward survival. If you believe you will survive and practice this attitude regularly you can enhance your ability to survive. The lesson here is that you must remember to tell yourself that you will never give up. Again, you *never* give up. You continue to fight no matter what the odds. If you receive an injury, and you feel pain, it means you are still alive. Pain is not a gauge of the severity of the injury, only a reminder that you need to continue to fight until you have won the confrontation. In this profession it is your job to win, so you must continue the battle to the end. Finish the fight and go home at the end of the shift. Remember that this is not high noon on Main Street where the Sheriff and the bad guy are going to meet to shoot it out. You must use whatever means are available to you, to win each and every encounter. So tell yourself every day when you leave for your tour of duty, "I will return home at the end of my shift. I will handle my calls with all the skills that I have learned, and if I am confronted I will win. I will do whatever it takes; bite, kick, punch or shoot, but I will fight to the end. I will never give up, I will not lie down and die and I will go home at the end of my shift. I owe it to my family, my co-workers, my profession, and myself."

Chapter 6
Finish the Fight[1]

An important component in survival skills is the ability to properly prioritize survival tasks when under stress. For example, cover and concealment, radio communications, and stopping the threat are important considerations in a gunfight. But in what order should they be prioritized? Obviously, this will depend partially on the circumstances of the incident. If you are under fire and very close to cover, you may choose to take cover and call for backup before returning fire. Or, you may take cover and return fire immediately if there is insufficient time to use the radio. Ideally, you may choose to return fire while moving to cover, provided that you are proficient in shooting on the move.

Unfortunately, not all law enforcement officers receive ample training, or practice time, in shooting and moving at the same time. This is where proper prioritizing of survival tasks becomes essential. If you try to shoot and move simultaneously without the necessary training and practice to do it well, you will probably not be very effective. You will be attempting to do two things at once and most likely not doing either one very well, or at least not as well as if focusing on one task at a time. To complicate matters, you have additional factors to consider that your assailant will most likely not be concerned with, such as the safety of civilians in the area, for example. These complicating factors make the prioritizing of survival tasks even more important, because they make it next to impossible for you to focus on one thing at a time.

How then, do you prioritize cover and concealment, radio communications, and stopping the threat? Every gunfight is different and there are too many possibilities to try to outline them all, so it is necessary to have guidelines to follow that can be applied in all instances. A basic rule of thumb is this: *Cover and communications are essential, but should be utilized only when it is tactically safe to*

---

[1] Lt. Jeffrey J. Hall (Ret.) Alaska State Troopers

do so. In other words, if moving to cover or using the radio will leave you more vulnerable to the attack, then your first priority must be to **Finish the Fight**.

This can be a difficult concept to embrace. It can go against your natural instincts. When under fire the instinct to get to cover, or to call for help, can be very strong. However it's important to remember that following your natural instincts will not always provide you with the best hope for survival. You must choose the course of action that will leave you least vulnerable to the attack, and give you the best chance of neutralizing the threat, thereby increasing your chances of survival. This may mean you will have to stand your ground and finish the fight.

In any case, finishing the fight and taking cover should take priority over using the radio to call for backup. Most gunfights last only a few seconds at most, so even if you do call for backup, chances are the fight will be over long before backup arrives. In the case of a more lengthy battle, it would be wise to call for help during a break in the action, just as soon as you can do so *safely*. Otherwise, radio communications may have to wait until the threat is over. Above all, you must be sure that using the radio, or moving to cover is done as soon as it can be done *tactically*.

Let's look at an example to illustrate the finish of the fight concept. Suppose you are conducting a vehicle stop for a traffic violation. As you approach the vehicle, the driver gets out and points a handgun at you. It happens so quickly that your sidearm is still holstered as you find yourself staring down the barrel of the weapon. You are standing with your patrol car to your right, and traffic to your left. This leaves you with a narrow path of mobility. You can move forward or backward, but your side to side movement is limited. What will you do?

You must prioritize survival tasks. Your first priority should be the threat. You must eliminate the source of the danger. Moving to cover will not accomplish this. Neither will calling for help. You are trained and equipped to handle a gunfight, and in this particular scenario that is exactly what you should do. Under a different set of circumstances, taking cover immediately may be your best option, but in a situation as bad as this, you must finish the fight. There's no doubt about the fact that this is a very bad situation to be in, and if it happens to you, you will be in grave danger. Regardless of the plan of action you choose, your chances of being shot are very real. The idea is to minimize the danger by properly prioritizing your survival tasks.

You may have heard the old saying, "You can't outdraw a trigger squeeze." In other words, if you are facing a subject with a firearm drawn and pointed directly at you, the simple fact is that you will probably not be able to draw your weapon and fire a shot before the subject can fire, *if* he or she chooses to do so. Everyone knows that action is faster than reaction and that certainly is the case here. This means that in these circumstances, you can expect to be shot at while drawing and preparing to fire.

The problem with this old saying is that it may leave you with the idea that drawing and firing is simply not an option under these circumstances. This belief can be dangerous. If you believe that using your sidearm is not an option, you are left with few choices. You may feel that your only option is to move to cover before drawing your weapon. Again, cover is an important consideration, and should not be discounted. The problem is that you may leave yourself vulnerable to being shot while moving for cover. Of course, you are also vulnerable if you stand your ground and return fire. Obviously, whichever option you choose, you will be shot at if that is the intent of your attacker. The question is, *which option leaves you more vulnerable?*

There are two main factors to consider in attempting to answer this question. The first thing to remember is that while moving for cover, you become a moving target, rather than a stationary one. This will hopefully reduce your chances of being shot. Unfortunately, this is really your only hope for survival if you choose this option. You have to count on the fact that while you are moving to a position of cover or concealment, your assailant will miss with every shot fired. This can be quite a gamble when you consider that even though you are now a moving target, your opponent can continue to give his full attention to his attack. Also, in this particular scenario, you will most likely be moving in a straight line away from your assailant while moving for cover. Your vehicle is limiting your movement to one side and traffic is restricting you on the other. This means that even though you are a moving target, you will not be as difficult to hit as if you were moving across your assailant's line of sight. Additionally, your attacker can, if he chooses, give chase while you move to cover, shooting at you all the while. All in all, you will be relying only on sheer luck to keep you safe while running for cover. The fact of the matter is that although you can't outdraw a trigger squeeze, you can't outrun it either.

This means that not only is drawing and firing an option, it may be your best option for survival. If you draw your weapon and fire, you can have a definite impact on your opponent's ability to successfully continue the attack. This can happen in one of two ways. First, if your bullets find their mark you can stop the attack. Obviously, this would be the ideal outcome to such a bad situation. Secondly, by returning fire you can force your assailant to take a defensive posture, thereby causing him to change his focus.

The Fight Plan

Just as a pilot has a flight plan, your assailant has a **Fight Plan**. It probably won't be very sophisticated. In fact, it may be nothing more than the determination to shoot you. Whatever the plan, your opponent will be focused on seeing it through. By drawing and firing at your assailant, you have the ability to change his fight plan. He may still be determined to shoot you, and may even continue shooting. But, now that you are shooting at him, he has other things to think about. He must now concern himself with such things as cover, and the fear of being shot. Naturally, if your bullets find their target, you will greatly improve your chances for survival, but even if you miss with your first shots, you can still adversely affect your opponent by changing his focus. He can no longer focus solely on shooting you. His life is now at stake, and he must divide his attention between offensive and defensive tasks.

By changing his focus from the offensive to the defensive, you change his fight plan and thus, his chances of being able to carry out his initial plan effectively. It has been said many times that shooting at paper targets on a firing range is not realistic training because the targets don't shoot back. This is one of the explanations given for the fact that even officers who shoot consistently well at the range often miss when under the stress of a gunfight. The same concept applies to assailants. Unless you're dealing with someone who is so detached from reality that he doesn't realize or understand that his life is in danger, shooting at him can place him under the same stresses that you feel when under fire. You may even gain tactical advantage by doing the unexpected, by fighting back.

What this boils down to is that most people do not enjoy being shot at, and as a result your assailant may be adversely affected. His accuracy and concentration may suffer. He may experience the effects of sudden stress syndrome, such as tunnel vision or auditory exclusion. Because he has probably not studied the effects of sudden stress, he will not be properly prepared. At the very least, as mentioned earlier, you will be forcing him to divide his attention between his original plan and defensive action.

Additionally, his Fight or Flight instinct will most likely come into play as a result of being shot at. If his flight instinct prevails, he may flee the scene, breaking off his attack and giving you the chance to re-engage tactically, with backup, for example. If his fight instinct takes over, you will have lost nothing. He was already shooting at you, and will most likely continue until you eliminate the threat.

It's important to remember that the adage mentioned earlier, "You can't outdraw a trigger squeeze" still holds true. In other words, chances are good that your assailant will probably fire the first shots in the gunfight. This means that during that split second or two while drawing and coming up on target, you are vulnerable to the attack. The important thing is that you are fighting back and not depending on your assailant's poor marksmanship skills for your own survival.

Chapter 7
Body Armor

I was working patrol one night around dusk and a car with only one headlight passed by going the opposite direction. I looked in the rearview mirror and I noticed that the car had a taillight out also. So I turned around and caught up to the car and made a stop. The car pulled over immediately. There were two people in the car, the driver and a passenger in the front seat. There was nothing at that point to indicate that anything was unusual. I walked up to the car and asked the driver for his license and registration and insurance. The driver was 19 years old, very polite, and didn't do anything to give me any cause for concern. He didn't have his license and the car was not his. He had borrowed it. He tried to open the glove box, but the handle was missing, so he got up on his knees in the driver's seat and turned around and started digging around in the back seat, looking for a screwdriver. While he was doing this, I got a good look around the inside of the car. I looked at the floorboards, front and back. He had a keg in the back seat of the car, and there were tools scattered all over the floorboards of the car. He found a screwdriver, and he turned back around and reached over and used it to open the glove box. He found the registration, but no insurance. So I wrote down his information on my note pad, and I went back to my patrol car. I ran the subject and started writing out the tickets while I was waiting for the return. It was taking a while, because a warrant had been located and it had to be verified. After a while the warrant was verified, but the only information on the warrant was that it had to do with a drug violation. I put my ticket book down on the passenger seat and I got out and went back up to the car. When I got to the rear window I told him that there was a warrant out for his arrest. I was still walking forward as I was talking to him. I couldn't see his hands so I took another half step forward. At this point, I saw the gun in his hand. He had it flat up against his chest. From the second I saw the gun, everything went into slow motion. At the same instant *that I saw the gun, I saw the muzzle flash. I never heard the shot. I never felt the impact of the bullet, but I was struck in the chest as I was trying to step back out of the way. I ended up out in the roadway about five or six feet away from the car. Luckily, there was no traffic coming. Everything sped up again and then I heard gunfire.*

I was on the ground at this point, rolling, trying to find some kind of cover, but there wasn't any. I had dropped my flashlight, and my hat had fallen off, and I didn't know where either was. During all this I could hear more gunfire. I counted a total of five rounds fired by the subject, including the one that hit me. I found out later that the guy had actually fired only three rounds.

At some point while I was on the ground I drew my weapon, and when I got to the other side of the roadway, I brought my weapon up and I was aiming at the rear tire of the vehicle, which was spinning. But I didn't shoot, probably because of the fact that there was a residential area behind the car.

After the guy drove off, I grabbed my flashlight and my hat and I went after him. I didn't put my hat on, and I didn't put my flashlight back in the ring. I didn't even holster my weapon. I just threw it all in the car and took off. I caught up with him and he lost control and ended up sideways across the road. He took off again and another half mile or so down the road he lost control again, and came to a stop. I stopped my car and when I got out, I had my gun in my hand, my hat was on my head, and I had my flashlight out, too. Sometime during the chase, I had holstered my weapon, put my hat back on, and put my flashlight back in the ring. I don't remember doing any of it, but I did. The driver took off on foot when the car stopped, but the passenger was still sitting in the car, so I had to secure him. I got him cuffed and put him in my patrol car.

Another officer, who was off duty, had seen the whole thing as he was driving by and had turned around and followed us down the road during the pursuit. He got there right after I got the passenger secured. After the other officer got there, and everything had calmed down a little bit, I leaned up against the car and I looked down. In the back of my mind I knew that I had been shot, but in all the commotion, I never had a chance to look to see if I was bleeding, or even to see where I was hit. When I looked, I saw the hole in my shirt, right in the center of my chest. That's when it hit me. I was shot. Luckily, I was wearing body armor that I had purchased with my clothing allowance money supplied by the department. The subject's weapon was loaded with .38 special +P rounds, and my body armor had stopped the round. I went to the hospital in an ambulance and I was released later that night. The subject was caught early the next morning.

The decision to wear, or not to wear, body armor is a decision which most officers feel is a personal choice. They are right of course, in that the decision whether or not to wear body armor belongs to them. However, the consequences of that decision can be far reaching. In deciding whether or not to wear your body armor, consider the following:

If you choose not to wear your body armor, you may not be able to provide good backup for your partner, or other officers, on the scene of a violent call. If you are shot, and not wearing body armor, it may be more difficult for you to continue the fight, and if you can't continue the fight, you will be leaving your fellow officers without backup.

The idea of leaving another officer without backup is unfathomable to law enforcement officers. However, most in the law enforcement profession think of this only in terms of abandoning another officer, or failing to engage in a fight, or even failing to respond to a call for help by another officer. An officer who would do these things would immediately be the subject of extreme criticism, which would follow him throughout his career. Yet law enforcement officers often neglect to wear their vests, never considering the fact that they may be placing their fellow officers at greater risk.

In addition to leaving your partner or fellow officers without backup, there are other consequences to consider. If you are out of the fight due to an injury, your fellow officers will now have the added distraction of your injuries to contend with. They may have a more difficult time focusing on the task at hand, due to their concern for your well being, especially if you are still in harm's way or under fire. In a high risk, high stress situation such as a gunfight, no one needs this kind of added distraction. Your fellow officers' chances for survival depend in part, like yours, on their ability to focus their full attention on stopping the threat.

As a law enforcement professional you have committed yourself to the protection of your fellow officers. You most likely take this commitment very seriously. Therefore, in order to ensure that you are able to fulfill this obligation, you must make a commitment to wear your body armor.

Additionally, you have sworn to protect the citizens that you serve. Imagine responding to a violent call such as a shooting, or a domestic violence call with shots fired. When you arrive, you encounter a situation in which a subject is firing a weapon at unarmed civilians. Naturally, your job will be to protect these people to the best of your ability. If you are not wearing your body armor you could be taken out of the fight before you have a chance to eliminate the threat. If this happens, the people depending on you will be out of luck. They will be at the mercy of the assailant, as will you. Again, in order to ensure your best chances of being able to do your sworn duty, you must wear body armor.

One of the most compelling reasons to wear body armor should be the protection of your own life. Obviously, if you are shot when not wearing body armor, your own life will be in great danger as well as the lives of your fellow officers and the civilians that you are there to protect. Additionally, there are other lives to consider when deciding whether or not to wear body armor. These are the lives of the people who would be most affected by your death. Your husband, or wife, would suffer a very untimely loss. You may have children who would have to go through the rest of their lives without a mother, or a father. Your parents and siblings should also be considered.

It seems lately that more and more officers are wearing their body armor consistently on patrol. However, this does not seem to be the case in other areas of law enforcement. Those who work plainclothes assignments typically do not include body armor as part of their duty equipment. There seems to be a tendency to equate body armor with the uniform. This does not have to remain true. Concealable body armor is designed to be concealed under clothing. There is no reason that it can't be worn under street clothes. Body armor manufacturers have made significant improvements in concealable body armor in recent years, making this more practical than ever before. In addition, body armor manufacturers are continually researching ways to make body armor even better. In the meantime, today's body armor is lighter, thinner, cooler, and more concealable than ever. Above all, it saves lives. The DuPont Kevlar Survivors' Club® registered its 2,500[th] save in May, 2000 (Police Chief Magazine, May, 2000.) Many of the body armor companies keep statistics on the number of saves their vests have to their credit. Unfortunately, these statistics have not been compiled into a comprehensive study recently. Not all vest makers use the DuPont product but these statistics should be impressive enough to convince nonbelievers to start wearing their body armor full-time.

Over the years law enforcement officers have come up with many different excuses for not wearing body armor. Let's examine some of these reasons closely.

"It's too hot."
Body armor can be hot; there's no doubt about that. Just *thinking* about putting on an undershirt, and body armor, and then a shirt, can be enough to make one perspire. If you add to this the extreme summer temperatures and high humidity in some parts of the country, it may seem unbearable. But this is not a problem that cannot be overcome. It is simply a matter of becoming accustomed to wearing body armor under these conditions. The only way to do this, of course, is to wear it every day. You cannot become accustomed to body armor if you do not wear it. It takes time. It's also important to remember that everyone's tolerances are different, and even when you do wear it all the time your individual level of comfort may still not be very high. In other words, it may never become comfortable, but it can become tolerable.

In extreme temperatures, it is important to stay properly hydrated, and this consideration becomes even more important when wearing body armor. If your working environment is hot and humid, you will no doubt perspire more with a vest than without one. Therefore, it becomes extremely important to drink plenty of water, sports drinks, or juice, during your shift. Remember that you have to stay hydrated for that foot pursuit that may come along unexpectedly.

"It's not comfortable."

Again, body armor can be uncomfortable. As mentioned earlier, the improvements made in recent years have made body armor more comfortable than ever, but it is still a long way from being as comfortable as that old T-shirt that you throw on after your shift. Remember what it is designed to do. In ancient times, knights did not wear suits of armor for comfort. They wore them for protection. Imagine the fate of a knight who decided not to wear armor because it was too hot, or too uncomfortable. He may as well have stabbed himself to death.

"It won't protect against head-shots."

As true as this is, it's still a lousy excuse for not wearing body armor. Obviously, you cannot make yourself bulletproof when you go to work every day. If you could, officer survival would be much less of an issue. As it is, however, you are susceptible to the damage that can be inflicted by firearms, and so you must do everything in your power to *minimize* your risk of serious injury or death. You do this by wearing your body armor. No, it won't protect your head, but it will protect your torso, which is a much larger target. Even if you are shot in the head, or another part of your body, which is not protected by body armor, you are not necessarily going to die. Remember that the idea is not to be bulletproof, but to tip the scales in your favor.

"It won't stop rifle fire."

Although body armor capable of stopping rounds fired from high-power weapons can be purchased, the body armor worn by most officers on a daily basis will protect the officer only against handguns. Here again, you can't make yourself invincible. The idea is to improve your chances of survival by gaining every advantage available to you.

"You're going to die when it's your time."

Obviously, everyone dies and it's only a question of when. However, if you subscribe to the idea that you will die when your number is up, and you are powerless to stop it, it may be wise to consider a career change. On the other hand, if you plan to be around to see your children grow up, you must believe that your fate lies, at least partially, in your hands.

"It makes me look fat."

This is by far the worst excuse for not wearing body armor. If you are in reasonably good physical condition, your vest will add a minimal amount of bulk. If you are not, however, the vest is not the problem. In fact, the larger you are, the greater the need for protection because you provide a bigger target for an assailant. If your vest will not fit under your clothing, then it will be necessary to either purchase larger size clothing, or increase your physical fitness program to reduce your size.

"It's in my car. I can put it on if I need it."

Occasionally, a situation arises that provides sufficient time for responding officers to stop and don body armor before arriving on scene. These situations, however, are the exception rather than the rule. Even then, there are certain considerations when you put your vest on over your clothing. If you have the time to stop and put on your vest, the situation may be unfolding in such a way that the suspect also has the advantage of time. If this is the case, the suspect will have the time to recognize the fact that you are wearing body armor, and may choose to aim for your head.

The main reason to wear your body armor under your clothing, as opposed to keeping it in your vehicle, is the fact that most shootings occur under conditions that do not allow you the time to retrieve your vest and put it on. Not having your vest on when you are in a life or death situation can have catastrophic results. You may be distracted by the realization that you are not wearing body armor in a life-threatening encounter. Obviously, when you are in imminent danger, you do not need *any* distractions. You must remain completely focused on stopping the threat. This particular distraction can be especially devastating, because it can increase your level of stress as you become aware that you are more vulnerable than you would be if you were wearing body armor. Remember the effects that an increased stress level can have on performance.

"I don't need it. I don't work patrol."

Even if you aren't assigned to patrol, you probably don't spend all day, every day, at your desk, at your assigned station. There is always work to be done in the field. Whether you are out looking for a suspect, tracking down witnesses, or even going to lunch, you will be exposed to potentially dangerous situations. You are, after all, on duty. You must be prepared to handle whatever situation comes your way. Your suspect may resist. Your witness may be in the middle of a domestic dispute when you arrive. The restaurant you choose for lunch may be the target of an armed robber. The point is, you cannot predict when you will become involved in an armed confrontation. By wearing your vest you can increase your level of preparedness.

Additionally, you cannot assume that you are safe when you are seated at your desk at the station either. Police stations have in the past been the scene of violent gunfights. In 1994, in Washington, D.C., a man walked into the Metropolitan Police Department and opened fire with a 9-millimeter pistol. Two FBI Special Agents and a Washington, D.C., Metropolitan Police Sergeant were killed. The subject also wounded an FBI Agent and a civilian. The assailant was wounded in the exchange of gunfire and committed suicide at the scene by shooting himself in the head. (Law Enforcement Officers Killed and Assaulted, 1994)

Other benefits of body armor

Body armor is designed to protect you in gunfights. It is not designed to protect you in motor vehicle accidents, or to offer protection from edged weapons. However, body armor has on many occasions been credited with saving officers' lives in a variety of situations not involving gunfire. Officers' lives have been saved by body armor in high-speed vehicle crashes, and in situations where an assailant has stabbed them. One officer was saved by his vest after being caught underneath a suspect's vehicle.

I was working graveyard and at the end of the shift two deputies were dispatched to a commercial burglary. They found evidence of entry and they secured the building to wait for canine. I headed into the area to see if I could assist. One of the deputies gave me a vehicle description and asked me to check the area. I checked the area and didn't locate the vehicle. At that point one of the other deputies advised on the radio that he had spotted the vehicle and was in pursuit. The vehicle wrecked and then continued down a ditchbank. We kept chasing him and he lost control and slid into the ditch. The vehicle came to rest on the driver's side. The subject climbed out the passenger window and stood up on the vehicle. He jumped across to the other side of the ditch and we went after him. He ran toward a known drug house where there was a truck parked in the driveway with a guy sitting in the driver's seat. He was there to make a buy. The subject jumped into the passenger seat of the truck. We started to advance on the truck with our weapons drawn. At this point a guy stepped out of the house and we ordered him to go back inside, which he did. I ordered the driver out of the truck and as I was dealing with him, our suspect slid over into the driver's seat. He started backing the truck up and as he went past, I could see the other deputy on the other side of the truck tumbling through the air. Then the guy stopped the truck and I had lost sight of the other deputy. I didn't know exactly where he was but I knew he was in trouble. I then got into a position in front of the truck to keep him from getting away. The guy put the truck in gear and I heard the wheels spinning and the truck began to move toward me. At this point I got tunnel vision. I fired one shot at the driver. I heard the shot but it didn't sound very loud. I saw and clearly heard the windshield break. The subject's head went back and then he leaned over in the seat. I didn't think I had hit him. After that, the tunnel vision went away and I saw the other deputies that had arrived to assist. I hadn't seen them before that. We got the guy out of the car and he was bleeding very badly. That's when I realized I had hit him. The other deputy got up and he looked pretty bad. His uniform was torn up and he was bleeding from his head. He ended up with two cracked ribs and several cuts and scrapes from being caught under the truck. According to the doctors, his injuries could have been much more serious if he hadn't been wearing his vest.

Here's another example of how body armor can prove to be very valuable even in an unarmed encounter.

I was working on a saturation patrol around midnight in an area where the wild parties had gotten out of control. There were about a dozen officers working the detail with about half of us on foot patrol. I was walking down one of the more crowded streets with a couple of other officers when an officer on the other end of the street got into a foot pursuit with a wanted subject. I listened to the pursuit on the radio and it was obvious they were coming right at me. I waited a few seconds and then I could see the guy heading toward me, right down the middle of the street in a dead run. I got in front of him and I could see that he was trying to figure out which way to go. There were patrol cars lining the street and other officers blocking his path so his options were limited. I guess he decided if he couldn't get around me, he would go over me, because he ran directly at me. I crouched low and braced myself so I wouldn't lose my balance when he hit me. He ran into me at full speed and I stopped him cold. His arms folded up in front of him and struck me in the chest. I picked him up off the ground and threw him onto the back of a patrol car where we cuffed him. Afterwards, I noticed that my chest was hurting, right in the middle, at the sternum. When I got home after my shift I took off my body armor and removed the shock plate. The shock plate had a noticeable dent in it from the collision. I was sore for a day or two, but that was all. It could have been much more serious if I hadn't been wearing my vest.

Another officer describes how his vest protected him when he crashed his patrol car.

I was on my way to back up another officer on an alarm call and I was running code. On the way, there was a vehicle that would not pull over to the right. I started to pass the vehicle on the right and when I did the vehicle went right, so I went back to the left. The vehicle in front of me went left also, and I had to go into the turn bay to avoid a collision. When the turn bay ended I was headed toward the median and I struck the median with the left wheels of my patrol car. I spun around and I got tunnel vision as I saw a huge tree that looked like it was coming right at me. The front of my vehicle struck the tree. My leg was broken and there was severe blunt trauma to my chest. The doctors told me that my heart was bruised and that the vest prevented my injuries from being more serious by spreading out the force of the blunt trauma across my chest. The force of the impact was so strong that the corner of the shock plate was actually bent where it started to fold over the chest strap of the seat belt during the collision.

As you can see, body armor is a very valuable asset for any law enforcement officer. It offers protection in a variety of situations. Its disadvantages are easily outweighed by its ability to protect you from serious injury or death. **A study by the FBI in 1998 showed that an officer is 14 times more likely to survive an armed encounter while wearing body armor.** The only way to take advantage of body armor's ability to save your life is to wear it. You can't predict life-threatening events, so you must be prepared for them.

Chapter 8
Off-duty Survival

Because you are a trained and experienced law enforcement officer, you are undoubtedly very aware of your surroundings and everything happening around you. As a result, your chances of becoming involved in a deadly force situation off duty may actually increase. Because of this, you have to be ready. You must give some thought to how you will react in an off-duty capacity should you be pressed into service. The level of action that you take when you are off duty and faced with a situation requiring law enforcement action should partially depend on a number of things that you would not normally consider when faced with the same situation when you are on duty.

Obviously, when you are off duty, you don't carry all the same gear that you carry on your duty belt. In fact, most officers carry only their sidearm when they are off duty. Some don't even carry their firearm, either as a matter of choice, or in compliance with departmental policy. Whether or not you are carrying your weapon should naturally affect your decision to act, or not to act, in an off-duty capacity. You certainly would be ill advised to confront an armed robber without a weapon. In this case, your best option would be to take the role of a good witness for responding officers.

When deciding whether or not to carry your firearm off duty, remember this: Carry your firearm **and** your badge, or leave **both** of them at home. Never carry one without the other. If you choose not to carry your sidearm off duty, don't carry your badge, or department identification, either. You wouldn't want to be caught in a situation, such as a takeover robbery with a badge in your pocket, and no way to defend yourself. Of course, if you do carry your weapon when off duty, you will need to carry your badge and department identification also, so that you can identify yourself to the suspects, as well as to any uniformed patrol officers who respond to the scene.

Even if you are carrying your firearm, you still must take into consideration the fact that you probably aren't carrying the rest of your duty gear. Any situation that requires law-enforcement action can require any level of law-enforcement action. When you are on patrol, you encounter situations that require you to intervene at various levels. In some situations your verbal skills and your command presence are enough to control the situation. In others, you may have to use other resources such as your chemical agent or your baton. Some situations may require the use of empty hand control techniques and possibly handcuffs. Still fewer situations require the use of firearms as a means of control.

Why then, do most law enforcement officers carry only a sidearm when off duty? For one thing, many officers try not to become involved when they are off duty unless they find themselves thrust into a situation that they feel requires immediate action. In many situations an off-duty officer can respond simply by calling for on-duty officers to respond to the scene and handle the situation. It is only the more serious situations that trigger an officer's training and instincts and cause them to become involved even when they are off duty.

This is why it is extremely important to give some thought to your off duty survival and tactics. When you are off duty and a situation arises that causes you to feel that you have to take action, you must ask yourself if it is absolutely necessary for you to become involved. Secondly, you must ask yourself if getting involved in this situation is worth the risks to your safety. Even if there are lives at stake, there is no point in becoming involved if you cannot gain some kind of tactical advantage. Otherwise, you could be seriously injured or killed, which would be of no help to anyone. Remember that your objective is to be helpful by winning the encounter, and not to become a hero whose name makes it onto the walls of the National Law Enforcement Officers Memorial.

According to the US Department of Justice, Law Enforcement Officers Killed and Assaulted, 1998 Report, 16% of all law enforcement officers killed in the line of duty from 1989 to 1998 were in an off-duty status. This number is significant enough to gain our attention. Just 1% should be enough to convince you that it can happen to you and that you must prepare a tactical plan of action in the way you equip yourself and respond to off-duty situations.

If you decide to become involved in an off-duty situation, you must think about the equipment and resources that you have available to you. Perhaps more important is to think about the equipment and resources that are **not** available.

The first and foremost resource that probably won't be available to you immediately is backup. Every officer knows the importance of backup. Yet many officers become involved in very dangerous situations off duty prior to the arrival of backup officers. Before becoming involved, ask yourself if you can wait for on-duty officers to arrive. Again, remember that your goal in this situation is to help those who are in danger. The on-duty officers are responding to assist you. If you get in over your head, you will then have to depend on them to get you out of trouble. Even though it may not be as practical as when on patrol, the same rule applies – always wait for backup.

Since you won't have your duty belt on, this also means you probably won't have any communications equipment. This presents another tactical consideration. How do you insure that backup will be on its way and that they will be able to identify you as an officer? This is why it is important to carry your badge with you if you are going to carry your firearm. If you have a cell phone or have someone else call for you insure that a complete description of you and what you are wearing is given to the dispatcher. It is also important for the dispatcher to know which agency you are with. Once the marked units arrive on scene, expect to be treated as a suspect and comply with the orders given. Once the scene is stabilized additional identification can be made.

Another very important piece of equipment is your bullet-resistant vest. Most officers don't wear a vest when off duty. A vest is more difficult to conceal in plain clothes, and most officers simply do not want to wear them when off duty. Even with the many advancements that have been made in recent years, vests are still somewhat cumbersome and uncomfortable. Most officers welcome their time off as a chance to escape the discomfort of the vest. To them, to continue to wear the vest off duty is unthinkable. This is certainly understandable. However, some officers do wear a vest off duty. This type of commitment to survival is rare. If you choose not to wear your vest when you are off duty, you must think about that fact when deciding whether or not to become involved. Remember that you carry your firearm in order to be prepared for a gunfight, and you can't be fully prepared for a gunfight without body armor.

Handcuffs are another piece of equipment that you may not carry with you off duty, but you probably should. Your experience and training tells you that situations can change very rapidly, and it is often necessary to de-escalate your level of force. Because you may not have your handcuffs with you when you are off duty, and because you probably won't have your chemical agent or baton with you either, your use of force options will be very limited. This is yet another good reason not to tackle a situation by yourself, if possible. Ideally, you should seriously consider carrying handcuffs off duty if you carry your badge and firearm. This will give you a force option between empty hand control and deadly force.

Another consideration in off duty situations is that even if you are carrying your firearm, you will probably be carrying it in a different type of holster than you normally carry it in. You may be carrying it in a smaller, more concealable holster. Or you may be carrying it in a fanny pack holster. The advantage to a fanny pack holster is that many of them are designed to carry additional equipment such as handcuffs or spare magazines. The disadvantage is that you may not be as proficient in drawing your weapon as you would be from your duty holster. This is true of smaller, more concealable holsters as well. If you do not train with them on a regular basis you may not be as proficient as you will need to be in a life or death situation. The old adage, "practice makes perfect" applies here.

If you are carrying your firearm in a holster, you may not have any additional magazines available should you need them. Also, if you are carrying your firearm concealed you must practice drawing it quickly. This is an area of survival that is receiving more and more attention. Training has recently become available in concealed carrying and drawing techniques. If you regularly carry your firearm off duty, it would be wise to seek out such training.

Additionally, you should consider what to do if you find it necessary to take some type of law-enforcement action when you are off duty and you are with family or friends. Have you discussed with your family members what they should do when the time comes? The members of your family should have a plan ready to put into action to insure their safety. Basically, there are two courses of action that they should be ready to take. First and most importantly, they must get to a position of safety. Once they have done that, then they can take steps to try to help you stay safe, such as calling 911 to insure that you get backup as quickly as possible. Also, they should know to give the dispatcher all of the pertinent information about the situation and about **you**. The on-duty officers that respond to assist you need as much information as possible about the crime and the suspects. Your family members should also tell the dispatcher that you are involved and they should give a detailed description of you so that the uniformed officers do not mistake you for a suspect.

Also, prior to becoming involved, remember that just because you're off duty and out of uniform doesn't mean that no one knows you're a law enforcement officer. Your awareness and alertness, while undoubtedly valuable to you, can also give you away. Additionally, the way you dress can also alert criminals to your presence. T-shirts with law-enforcement slogans, caps with miniature shoulder patches, and those fanny pack holsters, are just a few of the things that law enforcement officers wear that let everyone around them know who they are. If you choose to wear these things, the important thing is to remember that you may not have the element of surprise on your side. Criminals may be just as aware of your presence as you are of theirs.

Another very important consideration in determining when to become involved in an off-duty situation, is the safety of onlookers and bystanders. You will have to decide if intervention is in the best interest of the civilians in the area. In some situations it may be better to allow the criminals to complete the crime and take action afterward. However, if lives are in danger you may have to act immediately. This is **your** decision.

Chapter 9
Undercover Officer Survival

As with the off-duty officer, the undercover (UC) officer is faced with a variety of survival issues that are different from those of the patrol officer and most detectives. First of all, due to the nature of the work, the UC will probably not be armed, have a badge, nor have any of the normal law enforcement equipment. At most, the UC will have a pocket gun of small caliber, carried in a location that will make access difficult, to say the least. So how do you prepare yourself in the realm of officer survival if you are involved in a UC assignment?

One piece of protective equipment that you *must* have, when working undercover, is the surveillance / rescue team. The team should be armed with all of the necessary items and equipment needed to insure your survival. If a body wire is available it would be highly advisable to deploy it in the UC operation. This will keep the surveillance team aware of your status throughout the entire operation. As the saying goes "what can go wrong, will go wrong" so you must have a contingency plan, such as another UC within visual range, as well as "bust" signals and "trouble" signals that are both audio and visual. Additionally, the rescue team must have a preplanned course of action to be taken if you get into trouble. This is critical to your survival and you must maintain the attitude that you cannot do this alone.

As a successful undercover officer, you must develop the necessary skills for the particular assignment. You will need to have a working knowledge of underworld methods and the modus operandi of the targeted group. Your appearance and language will need to be compatible with the cultural background of the targets. You must insure that you are not known to the group or known in the particular area of the assignment. Also, you must be intelligent, self-confident, have good judgment and initiative, and excellent communication skills. Your survival skills will be dependent upon your ability to adapt to your surroundings.

The development of an undercover identity can be very important in the success of the operation and should be done carefully. Consider the following options:

Identity

When selecting an undercover name it would not be advisable to select the identity of actual people, living or dead, from your area. You should be sure that the name matches your ethnic background and it is a name you will alert to and remember. You may want to use combinations of names you know, like your mother's or spouse's maiden names, for example.

Background

In order to enhance your undercover role you will need to establish some personal background. Select a city that is very familiar to you and least likely to be known by the group you will be dealing with. You will have to choose schools, neighborhoods and employment scenarios that will be difficult to verify.

Documentation

You may also need some undercover documents to support your new identity such as a UC wallet and contents. This means you will have to obtain a driver's license, passport or immigration card, social security card, credit cards, bank accounts, birth certificate, business cards, etc. You will need to have sufficient documentation to keep up the facade.

Vehicle

Additionally, you must insure that the vehicle you are driving will not give you away during the undercover operation. Ideally, you should obtain a vehicle registration that matches the rest of the undercover identity you have established. You will also need to think about the type, make, and model of vehicle you will use, to ensure that it fits into the façade as well. You should also give serious consideration to the installation of a two-way radio, as this can become an officer survival issue if the radio is discovered. If you decide to have a radio installed, it would be highly recommended to select a style specifically designed for UC operations so that it can be well hidden.

All of these areas are important because, as you know, one slip and your cover is blown. If this happens, you will have to depend on your team and your skill to get you out safely.

Other Undercover Considerations

When conducting a UC operation, you will need to think ahead so you can plan the objective of the UC meeting. You must know what you want to gain from the meeting to insure you can control the situation. You will also need to brief the rest of the team assisting you with the operation. It does not matter if you are doing a UC buy, or a long and involved surveillance; the officer survival issues need to be addressed. If you currently do not use written operational orders you should consider using them as a means of mentally preparing all of the personnel involved in the operation. The written OP's order is an excellent way of ensuring that you do not leave anything out.

While conducting the undercover operation, make the suspects do what you want them to do without them knowing it. If you make them believe that something was their idea, or to their benefit, this can assist you in reaching your goal. Remember that you need to be in control, after all, the main objective is to gather evidence.

Also, when dealing with the suspects, remember that all conversation does not have to be about drugs or whatever the operation is covering. You should not present your entire cover story at once during the initial contact. Let this play out at a normal pace, as the suspects require information. Too much information at once can cause the suspects to become suspicious of you.

If you ask too many questions, or certain questions, during your contacts with the suspects, you may be setting yourself up to get burned. Do not ask specific or personal questions initially; allow the suspect to initiate this conversation. Pace yourself and remember that you will always be able to come back for additional buys or contacts, at which time you will be able to gather additional intelligence. It is also important to be a good listener during these conversations as you may receive information that is completely unrelated from that which you originally set out to obtain. As the conversation progresses you will want to remember names, dates, prices, telephone numbers and locations mentioned. This is where a wire will be beneficial, if you can get all of the conversation on tape.

During an undercover operation it may be necessary to use props in order to enhance your undercover role. These props can be anything, but most often will be things that help the suspect to believe you are not a law enforcement officer, such as an alcoholic beverage, for example. As an undercover agent you will need to control your alcohol consumption while actively conducting the operation for obvious reasons. Drinking an alcoholic beverage, such as a beer, during an undercover purchase of narcotics, and offering one to the suspect, can aid in establishing a connection or common ground. This is only one example. You are limited only by your imagination. You will also need to know how to handle requests to use drugs in the presence of the suspect. It is highly advisable that the only time this should be acceptable is when your life, or that of another, is in grave danger. The key here is to remember your limits as well as the officer survival factor to insure that when all is said and done, you leave the operation successfully.

There is obviously a great deal to consider when taking on an undercover assignment. You will have less equipment and resources available to you. You won't be wearing body armor, and your sidearm will be of a smaller caliber and carried in a different location. Even your demeanor must change when in contact with the suspects. For example, using the interview stance would surely blow your cover. In fact, most of the habits that you have developed when dealing with suspects must be pushed aside in favor of maintaining your cover. The exception is your survival attitude. It must be adapted to the situation. You must be constantly aware that as an undercover officer you are placing yourself at a serious disadvantage in many ways. This makes things such as mental rehearsal, physical skills practice, and the Finish the Fight concept even more critical to your survival.

Chapter 10
Critique

I was working an overtime assignment and I was dispatched to an area where two shooting victims were supposed to be located. Before I arrived, other officers had arrived and located a very drunken individual in the area. They thought that he might be the victim and so they stopped and checked on him. He was okay, so they got him up and sent him on his way. When I arrived, I asked dispatch for the phone number where the call had come from and I was able to find the pay phone where the call had been placed. I found an area that I thought might have been the area that the caller had described and I got out of my patrol car. I was walking down a ditchbank and I noticed two cars parked on the ditchbank a couple of hundred yards ahead. I then saw two people come from a wooded area and get into one of the cars. The car that they got into headed toward me on the ditchbank. There were two people in the car, a male and a female. I asked the male what he was doing there and he told me there were two people back there who had been shot, and he pointed in the direction of the other car. I told these two people to stay where they were and I continued down the ditchbank. As soon as I took two steps away from the vehicle I knew I had made a fatal error by leaving them there unsecured. I didn't know what was in the vehicle, or their involvement in the shooting, or anything about them. For some reason I felt at that point that I had to go to where the shooting victims were. I used my portable radio to give dispatch the license number of the car but I continued down the ditchbank. That tells me that I was aware of the mistake that I had made but for some reason I didn't go back and fix it. I found out later after the scene was secure that there were three fully loaded handguns in that car, all of which were within reach of the occupants.

Although self-critique can be very valuable after the fact, that is not the only time it is useful. It can also be very helpful during a call. Think back to your experiences during your field training, or on the job training. During this time you most likely continually evaluated your tactics to ensure that your training officer would approve of your tactical decisions.

As you gained experience you probably found yourself thinking less and less about your tactical decisions, and focusing more and more on the situation at hand. This is a result of becoming more confident in your decisions and abilities. This of course is beneficial because it allows you to focus more on the tactical aspects of the situation as a whole, rather than being distracted by individual details, such as your stance, or your positioning relative to your subjects, for example. These things have become second nature and are done with little or no conscious thought.

However, if you give no thought to your tactics during a call for service, you are more likely to make errors. Even the most experienced law enforcement officers should continually evaluate their tactics during all types of assignments. Law enforcement officers do make mistakes just like anyone else, and in law enforcement it is important to recognize our mistakes and to learn from them. It is even more beneficial to recognize mistakes as they occur and take steps to correct them immediately. If you remain constantly aware of your tactical options during all calls you respond to, and continually monitor your tactical situation, you can recognize a mistake, such as a bad position for example, and correct it **before** it becomes costly.

It is important to remember that tactical errors do not have to remain tactical errors. Mistakes can and should be corrected as soon as they are recognized. In other words, when you recognize a problem, fix it. Do not remain in a bad tactical position, or allow any tactical error to go uncorrected. This is essential regardless of whether the mistake is yours or another officer's. If you see another officer making a mistake that could be costly to anyone on the scene it is your responsibility to speak up.

Chapter 11
Tactical Terminology

Tactical terminology is terminology that instills the proper attitude necessary for the safe completion of a law enforcement task. Its importance lies in the fact that the words used to describe something can affect your attitude toward it. If, for example, you were told that during your next tour of duty you would be conducting routine traffic stops, you would probably not picture yourself using your patrol vehicle for cover, exchanging gunfire with the occupants of the stopped vehicle. You probably wouldn't picture yourself being struck by a passing vehicle either. You wouldn't picture these things because they are anything but routine. Yet they do occur during traffic stops, and you must be prepared. Why then, would anyone refer to traffic stops as routine? Almost no one does anymore. The term is still used in the media quite often, especially when something newsworthy develops from a "routine traffic stop." The term is simply not tactical. It implies that you are involved in an activity that poses little or no risk of physical injury. This can lull you into a false sense of security, leaving you less than prepared for a violent confrontation. You must remember that while not everyone you stop will be a violent fugitive from justice, nothing is routine; and nothing should be referred to as such.

The idea that your attitude and your approach to a situation can be affected by the term used to describe that situation is not new. Alfred Korzybski, a Polish-born American semanticist, first gave us the principle he referred to as "general semantics" in 1933, in a book entitled Science and Sanity: An Introduction to Non-Aristotelian Systems and General Semantics. Korzybski believed that words and behavior are interrelated, and that human behavioral responses can be improved through a more critical use of words. Ever since then, semanticists have been studying the relationship between words and behavior, using Korzybski's doctrine as the basis for their studies. It's not necessary for you to become a student of the Korzybski doctrine, or to become an expert in the field of general semantics in order for you to maintain a good tactical attitude. It's only necessary for you to understand that a relationship between words and actions does exist, and that words can have a distinct positive or negative effect on the way you approach your patrol duties.

First, let's take a look at an example of how words can affect us. If you're like many people, when you hear the sound of fingernails on a chalkboard, you may start to shudder or shiver. In fact, it's quite possible that you have experienced the very same reaction anytime someone even mentions the idea of fingernails on a chalkboard, or perhaps you shuddered just now as you read the words. This is just one example of how words can cause reactions within us on more than one level.

Another example comes from a study cited in <u>Eye Witness Testimony: Civil and Criminal</u>. In this study test subjects watched a simulated motor vehicle accident on film. When asked later about what they had seen, the responses changed according to the wording of the question. Those who were asked, "How fast were the cars going when they smashed into each other?" gave higher speed estimates than those who were asked, "How fast were the cars going when they hit each other?" Changing just one word in the question led to higher estimates of speed, even though all participants watched the same film. This, again, illustrates how words can affect us, many times without our knowledge. Now, let's examine a few of the different terms, both tactical and non-tactical, with which you are most likely familiar.

First, you know that there are two basic kinds of vehicle stops. The first type is a vehicle stop for a nonviolent offense such as a traffic violation. This is the type of vehicle stop that the media refers to as a routine traffic stop. You may have heard this type of stop referred to as a low risk stop. Of course, if you consider the fact that law enforcement officers are killed or injured during these vehicle stops every year, the level of risk could hardly be considered low. Regardless of the statistics, the fact that the potential exists for you to be killed during these vehicle stops is an indicator that you need to be cognizant of the danger involved. Therefore, the use of the term "low risk" is not much better than the use of the word "routine." The only reason it could be considered better at all is the fact that it does imply a certain amount of risk. But it does not accurately convey the level of risk you will be facing when conducting a traffic stop. For this reason, it cannot be considered a tactical term. If you think of traffic stops as "low risk," you may become complacent or lazy in your use of tactics. If you are then faced with a violent encounter, your chances of survival will be based on luck rather than skill and attitude.

It would be much more tactical to use the term "unknown risk" to describe the same type of vehicle stop. This term will help to instill in you the proper attitude necessary for conducting traffic stops safely. By thinking of traffic stops as unknown risk stops, you will be acknowledging the fact that every traffic stop contains a certain amount of risk, which can range from low to high. Since you won't know the exact level of risk you are dealing with, you will have to use tactics that allow for an immediate response to any threat that may present itself during the course of the stop. If all goes well, and you eventually send the violator on his way, you will have lost nothing. You will neither have wasted tactics nor have been overly cautious. You will have simply been prepared for the worst. This will prove to be very valuable if the vehicle stop goes bad. It also helps you to develop and maintain the proper tactics and the proper mindset for use on all of your future traffic stops.

If you approach all traffic stops of this type as unknown risk stops, the proper tactics will become habit. This, in turn, will increase your chances of surviving a violent encounter. It will also cause you to be more likely to continually reassess the level of risk that you are dealing with during traffic stops. You will be more alert to changes in the level of risk that may require you to make adjustments in your tactics. And, if you believe that any traffic stop can go bad, you will be mentally prepared, and you will not be taken by surprise if you are assaulted. If you are caught off guard, your reaction time could suffer. And the loss of even one second in a gunfight can be very costly.

The second type is a vehicle stop involving a situation where you have information that the subjects you are stopping have, or may have, committed a serious crime and may be armed and dangerous. It is commonly referred to as a "felony stop." A more tactical term would be the term "high risk stop." The term "high risk stop" is a very tactical term in that it accurately conveys the potential for danger that you face. It leaves you with almost no choice but to consider the stop a potentially life-threatening encounter and to select your tactics accordingly.

In physical skills training, such as defensive tactics, or firearms, you have probably heard a variety of terms used to distinguish between your right and left sides. Some of the more common terms used are the terms "weak hand" and "weak side," or "strong hand" and "strong side." These terms seem to be disappearing from training as more tactical terms are taking over. To use the word "weak" in training has negative connotations. It implies a weakness that you may not be able to overcome. The focus is not on your ability to use either hand well, but on the fact that one hand may not be as effective as the other, to the point of being ineffective. It may be true that if you are right-handed, you may not be able to use your left hand as effectively as your right, especially if you don't train equally with both hands. But that doesn't mean that the other hand is weak and you will be behind the power curve if you believe that it is. This belief can be especially damaging if you are injured in an attack and you're left with only one hand to neutralize your attacker.

During firearms training you have probably heard the term "support hand." This term is more tactical because it has less negative connotations. It does, however, lack positive connotations. It implies that the sole purpose of the hand is support; that without the strong hand it is useless. Still, it is preferable to the term "weak hand." Even the terms "strong side" and "strong hand" have some tactical problems. They may seem tactical at first glance, but to say that one is strong is to say that the other is weak.

The terms that are used in the medical profession, "dominant" and "non-dominant" are gaining acceptance in training circles; and you may hear them during training. These terms are more tactical because they have no implications whatsoever regarding the abilities of either hand. They simply acknowledge the fact that one hand is used more frequently than the other in performing certain tasks.

The term used to describe tactical training should be a tactical term also. You have probably heard either the term "Officer Survival" or the term "Officer Safety." The term "Officer Safety" seems to be gaining wider acceptance and the term "Officer Survival" is being used less and less. This may be due to the fact that the term "Officer Safety" is more "politically correct." It is a "softer" term that sounds less aggressive and less intimidating, and in today's world of community policing, softer terms are much more readily accepted.

It is not, however, tactical. "Officer Safety" is a term that brings to mind such things as wearing your orange vest while directing traffic, or wearing your seatbelt while driving. Of course, these precautions are important for safety; and it follows that to survive, you must be safe. The idea, however, is to use terms that will accurately convey to you the fact that your physical survival is at stake. The term "Officer Survival" does this quite well by being "tactically correct" rather than "politically correct." If you are trained in survival, as opposed to safety, you may as a result be more tactically minded. You will then be better prepared to handle a violent encounter, because you are thinking tactically.

Chapter 12
Tactical Thinking

One of the main lessons to be learned in everything covered so far is the need to think tactically at all times. You never know when or where your skills will be put to the ultimate test. Regardless of whether you work patrol, investigations, or any other law enforcement assignment, you can find yourself faced with a life or death encounter at any time. You must be mentally prepared for it.

When you are on duty, you must be constantly aware of all of the tactical considerations in every situation. You should continually monitor the circumstances to be aware of the tactical advantages and disadvantages that you may face. Cover awareness, number of subjects, availability of backup, and presence of weapons are all examples of items that must be considered. When a tactical disadvantage is discovered, the next step is to determine if the disadvantage can be corrected. If it can be corrected without sacrificing something else, then it should be corrected immediately. On the other hand, if the tactical disadvantage is something beyond your control, then you must simply be aware of it in case the situation turns bad.

It's also important to remember that there are very few situations in which there is only one possible course of action. As you know, thinking on your feet is essential in law enforcement. While you are continually re-evaluating your situation, you must be prepared to change your plan of action when necessary.

I was dispatched to a domestic dispute one night at around midnight. I arrived with another deputy and we approached the house. Dispatch had advised that there was a man threatening to kill his pregnant wife, and that there were children in the house as well. The house was a mobile home with a small wooden platform at the front door. The other deputy stood on the platform to the left side of the door. There wasn't room for both of us so I stayed on the ground level slightly to the right side of the door. He knocked on the door and when it opened, a male subject came out the door with his hand raised over his head. I could see a large-edged weapon in his hand. We both drew our weapons immediately and ordered him to drop it. He held the weapon over his head and it looked as if he was trying to get into a position where he would be able to stab the other deputy. I decided I had to shoot. At the time I was carrying a .357 revolver and I realized I did not have a safe backstop in case the rounds went through, or in case I missed. I didn't know where the guy's wife or kids were and I was concerned about shooting them accidentally. All of this went through my mind in a split second and I decided to move my sights from the subject's ribcage up to his head. I felt this would give me a safer backstop because of the angle I would be firing from. Since I was still at ground level and the subject was up on the platform, I figured any rounds that went through would be too high to strike anyone in the trailer, and would probably end up in the ceiling. Then I started to pull the trigger. As I was pulling the trigger back slowly, I ordered him one more time to drop the weapon. This time he complied and I was able to let the trigger go forward again without firing.

You must also remember that your tactical plan can be changed by the actions of another officer. There is not always time to communicate your intentions to your fellow officer, and when one officer commits to a course of action, you may have to adjust your plan accordingly. Always remember that not all officers on a scene may be planning on the same course of action. Another officer at a scene may do something that you are not expecting, making it necessary for you to change your plan. Equally important is the possibility that your actions can be unexpected by other officers as well.

Two of our officers on the graveyard shift were dispatched to a domestic dispute. A guy was reportedly armed with a knife and threatening several people. I happened to be close by, so I headed into the area. The two officers who were dispatched arrived first, and I arrived right after them. They had already confronted the subject in the street. He was holding a fixed-blade knife with a 4-inch blade. He was refusing commands to drop the knife. I was pointing my gun at him while the other two officers pointed their guns at him and continued to order him to drop the knife. We had him fairly well contained, leaving him only one avenue of escape, which was directly behind him. He could not have retreated back into the residence without going through one of us. My plan at that point was to continue with the commands until he complied. I didn't want to go hand to hand with this guy while he was holding the knife. I certainly didn't want to shoot the guy, but I wasn't going to risk getting stabbed, either. I thought the other two officers had the same plan. I was wrong. One of the other officers jumped the subject. I had no choice at that point. I holstered my gun and jumped into the fight. The officer who had jumped the guy had one hand on the knife and I grabbed for it also. I knew we had to get control of the knife or someone was going to get cut. Among the three of us, we managed to get the subject cuffed and under control without anyone getting hurt.

It is especially important to think about changes in your tactical plan if you are working with someone you are unfamiliar with. If you have a partner, you have probably become very familiar with each other and you can probably handle situations smoothly and quickly without very much verbal communication. This is a benefit of a good partnership. However, many officers work without partners, and even those that do have partners often work with other officers as well. This makes it necessary to be aware of the possibility of someone taking action that forces you to change your plan.

Another important consideration in tactical thinking is to never underestimate the people that you come into contact with during your duties. Not every criminal breaks the law with little or no planning, simply to support a drug habit. Many criminals actually take the time to plan before committing a crime. Some even practice the skills necessary to increase their chances of successfully completing their task, such as shooting.

One offender, by the name of Edwin Henry Waltke, Jr., even wrote a sort of how-to manual for other criminals to follow. Waltke was involved in a shootout with police officers in North Las Vegas during a suspicious vehicle check. A reserve officer was shot three times and Waltke was shot four times in the exchange of gunfire. Afterwards, a search of Waltke's vehicle turned up the manual. In the manual Waltke discusses tips for selecting getaway cars, and stealing cars. He covers tips for conducting robberies and discusses the common ways that criminals get caught. He even discusses what he refers to as "combat rules," suggesting that an offender "use one opponent as a cover and both in line, if possible." He also advises other criminals to be aware of plain-clothes officers. He writes "A wise fugitive looks for plain-clothes cops and recognizes one about as well as the cops recognize him. The first to be convinced has the advantage." Waltke is just one example of a well-prepared criminal and an excellent reason to remember to never underestimate the people you meet in law enforcement. Offenders like Waltke also serve to remind us of the importance of tactical thinking in all aspects of law enforcement.

Moreover, tactical thinking is just one element of Tactical Attitude. Tactical Attitude is about who we are as peace officers. It is about our way of life. It is about our commitment to our profession and it is about our commitment to **survival**. An experience of one of the authors, Dennis Nasci, defines Tactical Attitude. In this situation there are examples of many topics covered. Most important is the fact that when law enforcement officers think tactically, remain alert, and use every advantage available to them, a potentially violent situation can end safely.

> *I was working swing shift in our south patrol area as the watch sergeant. Two of my deputies received a domestic violence call that caught my ear so I rolled on the call as well. When we got there the woman said she was bringing the kids back after her weekend visit. The ex-husband had invited her inside but she declined. He then became very angry and started to come after her so she got back inside her car and locked the doors. He broke out the driver's window and at the same time she escaped out the passenger door, running to a friend's house to hide. When it was safe, she got a ride home. She lived on the same street, about ¼ mile away. Once at her apartment her ex-husband came over and sent one of the kids up to the door in an attempt to get her to come outside. She wouldn't come out, so the ex-husband started breaking out all of the front windows, including the neighbor's windows, and the neighbor called us.*

At this point we obtained all of the information we could about the ex-husband and his residence. As we arrived at the ex-husband's residence, we learned that he had several weapons and was probably waiting for us. I found out that the victim had called him prior to our arrival and told him that she had called the police, and that we would be coming to take him to jail and take his kids away from him.

I had requested an additional deputy and I felt the four of us would be enough to handle this call. I then briefed my deputies on how we would approach the home and assigned one of them on point with me as his cover and the other two were to follow and take up a position to cover the rest of the area. As the point deputy moved from our covered approach to a vehicle in the driveway, I heard what sounded like the action of a shotgun. I made hand motions for all of the deputies to hold their positions, and I notified my radio room to clear the air and informed them that we had one subject armed with a shotgun. I also advised any additional units in the area that were available, to respond to the area but to stay clear of the driveway and other potential fields of fire.

The deputy on point called out in an attempt to make verbal contact with whoever was hidden in the shadows of the carport where the sounds came from. As the deputy talked with the guy they went back and forth about who would put their gun down first and he convinced the subject to come out after putting his weapon down. Once he was out in the open we were able to make a visual inspection and approach the subject who was later identified as the ex-husband. Separating us from him was a five-foot chain link fence with a locked gate. I noticed the guy's hand was bleeding and I asked to see his hand so I could check it out. The whole time I was thinking, if I could grab his hand I would be able to trap it between the panels of the gate until my deputies could get over the fence and secure him. At the last second he pulled his hand away. At this point, I learned that the key to the gate was in the house. He then said he would let one of the deputies over the fence to escort him to get the key. I let the deputy start over the fence knowing he would start to detain the subject as the rest of us made our way over the fence to assist.

As the deputy started over the fence, the guy made a beeline toward the back of the carport with my deputy in pursuit. I then saw him lean and grab something. I responded by drawing my sidearm and coming up on target as I moved to my left for a better field of fire. As I did this, I observed the outline of a Colt 45 in his right hand. I was sure of the weapon as it had a very distinct look, and at the time that was also what I was carrying. As I watched my front sight I started to press the trigger, and I made the decision that I would shoot when he brought the muzzle of the weapon around just short of my position. I started to narrow my concentration on the front sight as I was about 40 feet away and had a deputy moving into the field of fire. It seemed as if I had all the time in the world, not just a second or two. I kept telling myself to wait until he turned to my preplanned position. I planned how many rounds I would fire and where they would be placed. As I was reaching the point of no return on the trigger press and waiting for the round to fire, my deputy crossed my field of fire. To my surprise I pulled up and away without thinking and the round did not fire. At this point the deputy reached across the subject and stripped the weapon from his hand so hard that it went flying to the back of the carport breaking the bottom plate of the magazine allowing the rounds to fall out of it. Again without thinking, I had my weapon in the holster, snapped, and I was over the fence and on top of the subject assisting the deputy with cuffing him.

Near the suspect we found a Mac 11 (9mm) with the sear worn down allowing it to fire fully automatic. It had a 30 round magazine in the weapon and an additional 30 round magazine next to it. The Colt 45 had six rounds in the magazine, but nothing in the pipe. The sound I heard was the slide going forward on the Mac 11, not a shotgun.

During our debriefing of this call later that night several things came out that were very interesting. The first thing that we brought up was the initial intelligence. Had we not learned about the phone call made by the victim we may have handled our approach in a different manner. Because our agency had recently experienced several shooting incidents due to poor vehicle placement, we made our approach tactically. One of the senior deputies that responded to the scene later admitted he would have driven into the driveway and headed straight to the door. This could have been a fatal error and this senior deputy knew it. He reacted to this eye opener by modifying his approach tactically after this incident.

The second thing discussed was when I advised dispatch about the shotgun. The radio personnel heard what I said but took it to mean we were being shot at. They were confused because my tone of voice did not reflect our being shot at. They were also privy to all the same information we had, because we had relayed everything via radio. The responding deputies heard me say I had one subject armed with a shotgun but the dispatcher's response added to their sudden stress response. Additionally two of the deputies with me did not hear the action noise, but for me it sounded like I was right next to the weapon.

The next item mentioned was the deputy that went over the fence. As the subject took off running towards the back of the carport, he gave chase. As he reached the subject he saw the gun and drew his sidearm to a weapon retention position. He said that he then started to have an argument with himself as to whether he should shoot the subject or take the weapon away. He said he thought, "Should I shoot, or should I take the weapon away? I think I can get the gun. No, I better shoot." He said this went on for what seemed like several minutes before he decided he could get the weapon before the subject could shoot.

Last, I was doing what I was taught by watching the front sight and squeezing the trigger, waiting for the explosion. I knew I was very close to the end of the trigger squeeze and I had already planned my second shot. Although I was about

40 feet away I had what appeared to be a very large target area. I was experiencing a slow motion effect as well as time and distance distortion. In addition to all of this I was also starting to get tunnel vision, with all my concentration on the front sight and target. As the subject neared the point of no return (the predetermined point I was going to allow him to turn with the weapon) my sight narrowed further. This caused a problem when I did not see my deputy until he crossed the muzzle of my weapon.

I use this example to illustrate that in any encounter you can experience Sudden Stress Syndrome. To what extent you experience the effects can vary from one encounter to the next. In this example you can see several effects of Sudden Stress Syndrome as well as many other topics discussed in this book. I believe that due to my training I was not only able to recognize the effects of Sudden Stress Syndrome, but I was able to respond to them as well. I also want to point out that muscle memory came into play in this incident. Drawing my weapon, coming up on target, and holstering and securing my weapon, are just a few examples of the role that muscle memory played. Additionally, mental rehearsal was very beneficial. I had gained experience that prepared me for this incident, in practical exercises and real life experiences, as well as from the use of mental rehearsal, or the "what would I do if?" exercises.

The last thing I would like to stress about this particular encounter is the importance of the debriefing that was conducted. I feel this part of our training is most often forgotten, even though it may be the most valuable tool we have to learn from. There is not a set rule regarding how this type of debriefing should be conducted. It can be very informal, or very structured. I would suggest that for minor encounters a quick debriefing should be done, even if you are the only one involved and present for the debriefing. Evaluate what went wrong, and what went right, and come up with ideas of how you can do better next time.

At the risk of being redundant I would like to reiterate that you have a responsibility to your family, your profession, and yourself to win each and every encounter, whatever the level of risk. You are expected to go home at the end of every shift so you may return for your next tour of duty. Law enforcement needs professionals like you, so please remember that you owe it to yourself, your family, your agency, and your profession to go home at the end of every tour of duty. Think tactically, and be safe.

Bibliography

<u>Street Survival: Tactics for Armed Encounters</u>
Adams, McTernan, and Remsberg
Calibre Press, copyright 1980

<u>Deadly Force Encounters</u>
Dr. Alexis Artwohl, Loren W. Christensen
Paladin Press, copyright 1997

<u>Sharpening The Warrior's Edge</u>
Bruce K. Siddle
PPCT Management Systems, Inc., copyright 1995

<u>Eye Witness Testimony: Civil and Criminal, Second edition</u>
Loftus & Doyle
The Michie Company, copyright 1992

<u>The Nature and Conditions of Learning</u>
Howard L. Kingsley
Prentice-Hall, Inc., copyright 1957

<u>Essentials of Psychology</u>
Douglas A. Bernstein, Peggy W. Nash
Houghton Mifflin Company, copyright 1999

<u>Horror, Fright and Panic</u>
Hyde & Forsyth
Walker Publishing Co., copyright 1977

<u>The Psychology of Fear and Stress</u>
Jeffrey A. Gray
McGraw-Hill Book Co., copyright 1971

<u>Science and Sanity: An Introduction to Non-Aristotelian Systems and General Semantics</u>
Alfred Korzybski
International Non-Aristotelian Library, copyright 1933

Language in Thought and Action: Symbol, Status, and Personality
Samuel Ichiye Hayakawa
Harcourt Brace Jovanovich, copyright 1963

Killed in the Line of Duty
U.S. Department of Justice, Federal Bureau of Investigation, 1992

Law Enforcement Officers Killed and Assaulted
U.S. Department of Justice, Federal Bureau of Investigation, 1994, 1998, 2000

Police Chief Magazine, May, 2000

National Law Enforcement Officers Memorial Fund, 1999

Index